Following the
LEWIS AND CLARK TRAIL

A VACATION GUIDE
FOR CAMPERS

By

Doten Warner

Library of Congress Catalog Number: 97-95096

ISBN 0-9662609-0-2

Perseverance Publishing
15116 15th Street
Lutz, FL 33549

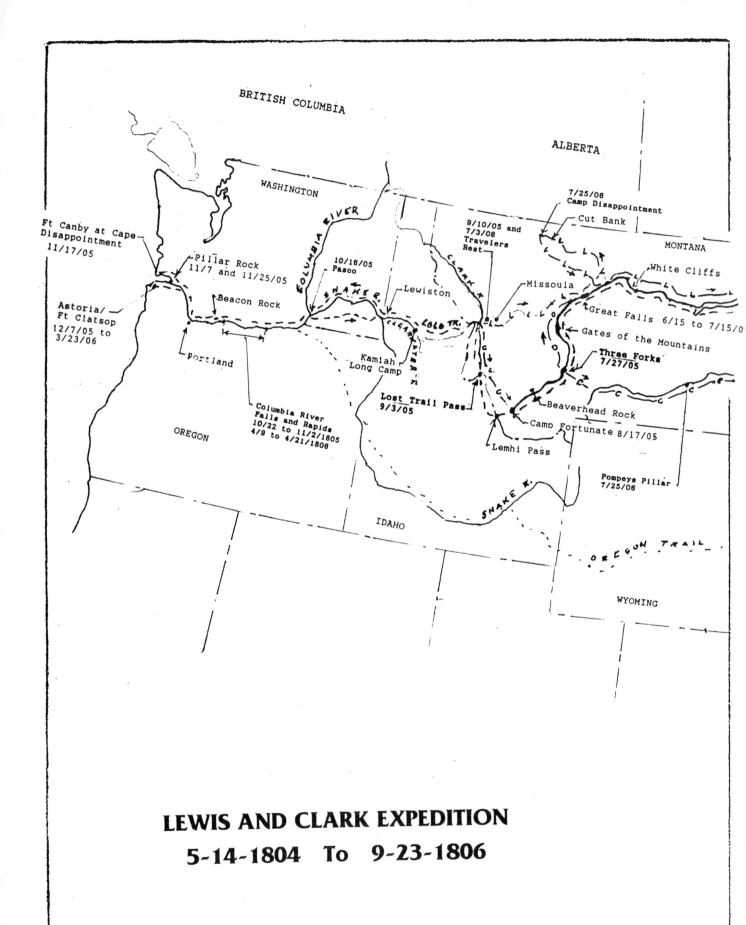

BRITISH COLUMBIA

ALBERTA

WASHINGTON

7/25/06
Camp Disappointment

Cut Bank

MONTANA

Ft Canby at Cape
Disappointment
11/17/05

Pillar Rock
11/7 and 11/25/05

COLUMBIA RIVER

10/18/05
Pasco

SNAKE R.

9/10/05 and
7/3/08
Travelers
Rest

CLARK FK

White Cliffs

Astoria/
Ft Clatsop
12/7/05 to
3/23/06

Beacon Rock

Lewiston

Missoula

Great Falls 6/15 to 7/15/0

LOLO TR.

CLEARWATER R.

Gates of the Mountains

Portland

Kamiah
Long Camp

Three Forks
7/27/05

Columbia River
Falls and Rapids
10/22 to 11/2/1805
4/9 to 4/21/1808

Lost Trail Pass
9/3/05

Beaverhead Rock

OREGON

Lemhi Pass

Camp Fortunate 8/17/05

SNAKE R.

Pompeys Pillar
7/25/08

IDAHO

OREGON TRAIL

WYOMING

LEWIS AND CLARK EXPEDITION
5-14-1804   To   9-23-1806

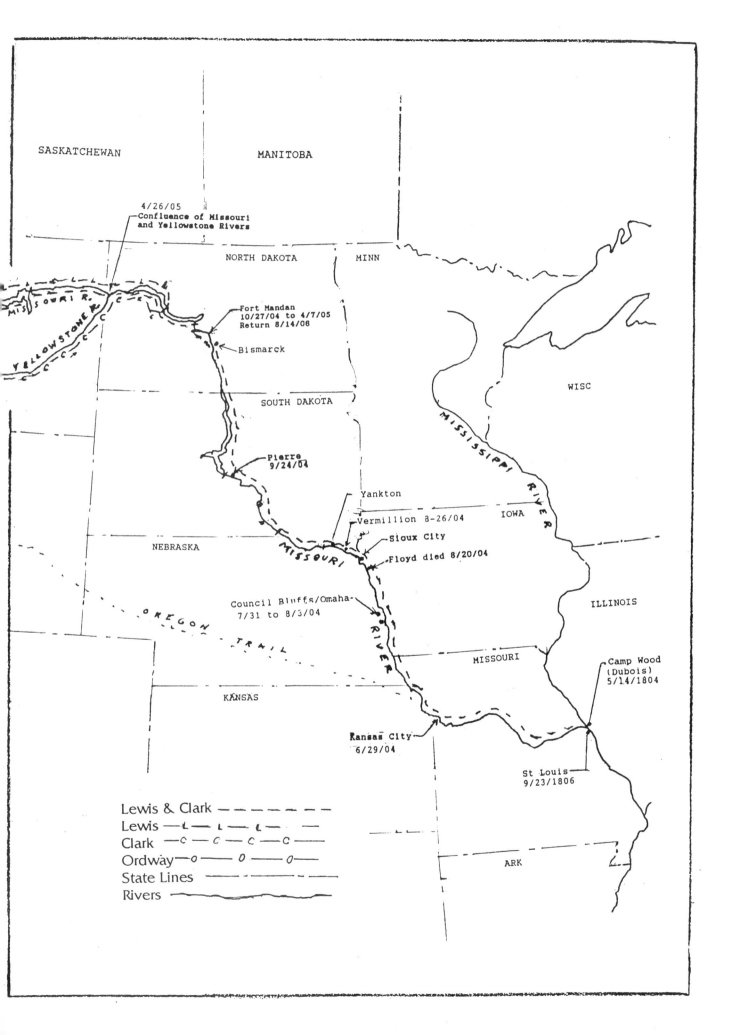

FOLLOWING THE LEWIS AND CLARK TRAIL
A Vacation Trip For Campers

INTRODUCTION

If anyone is looking for a great way to have a vacation, especially if you are campers, this story might appeal to you. And for patriotic Americans it is a reminder of what less than 50 admirable Americans did for their country almost 200 years ago.

This is really a report on the activities of Meriwether Lewis and William Clark and of the other members of the expedition that I discovered when reading their diaries. I am not a true history writer, for I have spent my life writing only building specifications and instructions for building airplanes, besides making drawings for the same. But I have been fascinated by the expedition of the Corps of Discovery, and for some reason not wholly clear to me, I started writing notes as I read the journals. This has gradually resulted in the following report, which has no fiction in it. I believe that history is served in a detrimental way by writers who mix history and fiction when they do not tell which is which. But, because the Lewis and Clark Expedition is so incredibly interesting, maybe this will be more than a dry set of specifications.

I have added maps you may refer to as the explorers' voyage advances, both outbound and on the way home. This may make the book a sort of guide. The dates on the maps correspond to the dates in the text, which are mostly in sequence. Wherever you are on the trail you can find what the explorers were doing as they passed that area.

When my wife, Lena, and I first crossed the Lewis and Clark Trail, it was in 1982, newly retired, and we were on our way up the Pacific coast on our way to Alaska. We were almost to the Columbia River when we saw signs that told us to turn here for Fort Clatsop, Lewis and Clark's winter quarters in 1805 and 1806. We stopped and saw a movie starring Lorne Green in a narrative of the Lewis and Clark trip. Since then we have visited many places all across this beautiful country of ours that were first visited, after the Indians, by those two captains and their incredible crew.

Campers that set out on a trip lasting a month or two, have to set priorities about where to go. That's a tough decision, but if they don't have some sort of a theme for the trip, a lot of places can be missed. Some campers leave home not caring where they are going; they just want to relax. But relaxation can turn to boredom quickly. A trip with a purpose can be more rewarding. One summer we visited the battlefields of the Revolutionary and Civil Wars.

They are well worth visiting because they remind us of the suffering and dedication of the combatants that formed our country's future. Another year we followed the Santa Fe and Oregon Trails. Both of those, like the Lewis and Clark Trail, expanded our country beyond the Mississippi River. We like following the Lewis and Clark Trail best because it is certainly not depressing like some of the others, but uplifting. We can read from the Corps of Discovery journals as we go along, and realize what it all looked like in its primeval condition, and rediscover it for ourselves.

There is one sure way to thoroughly enjoy following any of the western trails. That is what might be called the psychological approach. The Indians called it "walking in the other man's moccasins for a day," or "tread the path he trod." The dictionary says that empathy means "the ability to enter fully into another's feelings or experience." Maybe it is because I have empathy for the men of the Corps of Discovery that I have enjoyed following their path so much.

The uniqueness of the Lewis and Clark Expedition came to me as I read <u>A Short History of the United States</u>, by Nevins and Commager, 1945 edition, which says that the Lewis and Clark exploration has been called "incomparably the most perfect achievement of its kind in the history of the world." The more I read about the expedition the more I am impressed with the accuracy of that statement. Its level of perfection was like the perfection of the 1969 trip to the moon; enough to be extremely successful.

Most of the stories of the settling of our country are about hardship, fighting, and death. About wars and unhappiness. They make interesting stories because, like most drama, they have violence for their main ingredient. But the Lewis and Clark exploration of 1804, '05, and '06, with the exception of one tragic dawn when two thieves were killed, is the story of how about 33 peaceful people prevailed against the wilderness and had fun doing it. One died from appendicitis early in the 2-1/2 year trip, but the rest finished the expedition together, all healthy, and remained lifelong friends.

The diaries of the men of the Corps of Discovery tell about comradeship, excitement at seeing new landmarks, satisfaction about their progress, "inexpressible joy" at seeing a prairie on the west side of the mountains, much mirth when seeing Indian women "sitting promiscuously in the lodge," and "much jollity" when playing the fiddle, and the whole troop dancing for the natives.

It was a scientific expedition, and the plotting of the rivers and mountains with latitude and longitude all the way to the Pacific was something our country really needed. The botanical specimens which they brought back were studied the world over. They recorded in detail the political structure and the family life of each village through which they passed.

2

They tried very hard to get the tribes to stop making war on each other and they were sometimes successful, especially with the Mandan and Nez Perce people, for a long time afterwards.

Probably the most interesting thing to remember about the Lewis and Clark Expedition is that it was a race. It was a very serious race for the government of the new United States of America, for two reasons. First, the land on the Pacific coast was up for grabs to whoever got there first to claim it. The second is that both the U.S. and Britain believed that there was a shorter route for the lucrative China trade somewhere in "them thar hills." It had been a race since 1783 when Jefferson tried and failed to get General George Rogers Clark (William's brother) to explore as far as the Pacific. He found out that Britain was going to do the same thing, but ostensibly "only to promote knowledge," not to colonize. By the time Lewis and Clark got to Oregon, the British were not far behind, having developed a route north of the present U.S.-Canadian border. However, the British were having trouble descending the western rivers, and the Corps of Discovery were the first to reach the Pacific coast.

The expedition had been planned by Jefferson before the Louisiana Purchase, for even before his inauguration in 1801, he hired Lewis as his secretary, so that the two could secretly plan for the trip. The events leading to the planning, Lewis's efforts at getting supplies together and boat building accomplished, and his trip down the Ohio River to meet Clark is a story in itself. The Louisiana Purchase was a development in 1803 that took some of the need for secrecy from the project.

What impresses readers of the diaries of the 5 or 6 of men who wrote, is the dedication of the men to the mission, to their 2 officers, and to the president who sent them. They were all handpicked men who were mentally and emotionally equipped to strive together in the wilderness. Their two captains seem to have been preparing for this unusual journey since they were born, and even before that, because of their ancestry. Their families were prominent in the early development of our country, bringing up their children with the values of our founding fathers. Both Lewis and Clark were men of the army but their methods of leadership were more fatherly than military. They can rightly be ranked with Jefferson and Lincoln as "Men of the Century" for their contribution to our country's greatness.

It is interesting to contrast the record of this expedition with the records of other expeditions; the Oregon, Santa Fe, Gila, Old Spanish, California, and El Camino Real trails. Death on those trails was expected, and realized in sad quantities. No other leaders, except perhaps Fathers Kino, Garces, and Serra, leaders of the southern trails, had such loving and caring control over their men as Lewis and Clark had. The Santa Fe Trail, mainly used for freight, had travelers bent on making money, while the Oregon Trail had travelers whose main purpose was getting to the other end in one season. They formed a group mainly for security reasons. This lack of mutual support may be why the trail was littered with graves. On the Lewis and Clark expedition, no one was ever left behind, for their sick were carried and doctored as they went. During hungry times the hunger was mutually shared.

The Lewis and Clark story is not one which has one dramatic climax at the end; rather, it has many climaxes. In 28 months they reached different goals, and each had its climax. I hope you enjoy reading about each one.

Chapter 1

ST. LOUIS TO THE DAKOTAS
May 14, 1804 to October 27, 1804

THE START

A good place to join the Lewis and Clark Trail is at the Great Arch in St. Louis, Missouri. Remember that it was built to commemorate the Lewis and Clark expedition, besides the Louisiana Purchase. After you take the trip up the arch, be sure to go down into the museum to see an interesting portrayal of the expedition. Then drive north out of the city a short way, to where the Missouri River empties into the Mississippi, and you will notice that it is hard to tell which river is the largest. If, beyond this point, the Missouri had been named the Mississippi and vice versa, then the Mississippi would have been the longest river in the world instead of the Nile River, which has that distinction. If you drive upriver for a few weeks, you will begin to see how long the Missouri really is. Can you imagine what guts it would take to paddle upstream its entire distance?

Cross the Mississippi River on I-270 to the Illinois bank, turn north on Rt. 3, and three miles upriver there is a road on the left marked "Lewis and Clark Memorial." There you will see a cluster of monuments built by the 11 states that were discovered or partly mapped by Lewis and Clark. Why were they built at that particular place? Because that is Camp Dubois

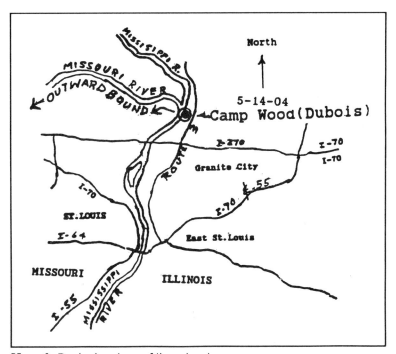

Map 1: Beginning days of the adventure.

(dubois is the French word for wood), where the expedition trained the winter before they set out May 14, 1804, paddling across the Mississippi and up the mouth of that wide Missouri. That spot is also where they officially ended their trip 2 years and 4 months later.

The first two days of their journey, until they reached St. Charles, Missouri showed

Captain Clark and the men the difficulty that they were going to have passing submerged trees and sand bars. At St. Charles there was a delay for almost a week while they waited for Lewis to arrive on horseback from St. Louis, about 20 miles. He had been detained to complete the expedition's business arrangements.

If you wish to see a replica of their 55 ft. boat, 'the barge', there are two of them that we have seen. In St. Charles there is a beautifully varnished replica built by Glenn Bishop, and he will be glad to show it to you. He has installed a motor, and in 1996 he retraced part of the 1804 passage of its predecessor. This replica has already become famous in its own right, because it won first prize in the 1992 Columbus 500 year commemoration parade in Washington, D.C.

> **Note:** Sadly, this replica of Glenn Bishop's 55 ft. barge was burned up in January, 1997 when his storage building in which it was stored, caught fire and all contents were destroyed. Glenn is now in the process of rebuilding it, along with replicas of the red and white pirogues that accompanied the expedition.

Each year in May in St. Charles, along the waterfront, there is a reenactment of the ceremonies that commemorate the transfer of the Louisiana Purchase from Spain and France to the United States. It is quite an interesting ceremony, with over a hundred actors in the colorful period uniforms of each nation. Lewis was in the 1804 ceremony at St. Louis, so his part is in the reenactment each year. There is a good campground in St. Charles so that campers can enjoy the festivities without doing a lot of driving.

Also in St. Charles is an educational Lewis and Clark Museum, run by Mimi Jackson, who can answer any question about the Lewis and Clark expedition. Last year she gave courses to 11,000 school children about the Lewis and Clark story.

St. Charles is proud of the fact that Meriwether Lewis joined the boats for the first time in St. Charles on May 20th. I doubt if the city is proud of the Corps' discipline problems that surfaced the first day the boats reached St. Charles. The Corps arrived at noon on May 16th, and there apparently was a Ball in town that some of the crew attended, 3 of them without permission. On the next day an enlisted men's court martial was held and sentenced Warner and Hall to 25 lashes, however, their former good conduct got their punishment remitted. Collins, though, got the full punishment when he returned to the boats at night because he had behaved 'unbecomingly' at the Ball and shot off his mouth about official orders. Clark was getting his men straightened out right at the beginning of the expedition. On Sunday, May 20th, they attended a Catholic Mass at the church. The next day all were back in the boats on their way upriver.

ON TO KANSAS RIVER

If you drive a few miles up the Missouri River, you can visit the home that Daniel Boone built when there was not enough wild country left in Kentucky for him, near the end of his life. He was 70 years old when Lewis and Clark paddled by. His advice had already been helpful to them. He died in 1820. His homestead is in Defiance, Missouri, which is now a very interesting museum, and was well worth the drive through farm country to see. Near there, on May 25, 1804, the Corps of Discovery passed the last settlement, La Charrette, a village of seven houses.

The beginning of their trip did not go well. In the first few days Lewis fell 20 ft. from a 300 ft. cliff but caught himself on the way down. The boats came very near to upsetting in fast currents due to inexperience. On one occasion the boat broke its tow rope and "She wheeled and lodged on the bank below as often as three times before we got her into Deep water." They lost two miles with that mishap. They found out that the boats should be loaded heavier in the bow when going upstream, for when they hit a sandbar the boat wouldn't be twisted around and go broadside to the current. On June 2nd, the Corps camped near to where Jefferson City is now. Drewyer (Drouillard) and Sheilds, who were bringing along the horses by land, had trouble keeping up with the boats because of swollen creeks and rivers

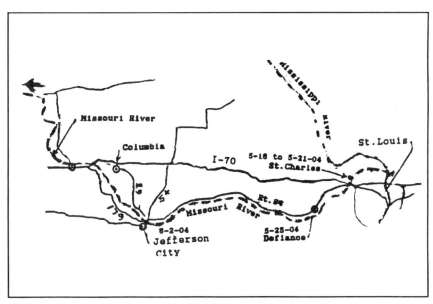

Map 2: Early inexperience made the going tough in the first days.

that entered the Missouri River. They finally caught up after a week of struggling. Near present day Boonesboro, Missouri the crew encountered a den of rattlesnakes. Many began to get boils, and the mosquitos and ticks became troublesome.

But they ate well. Game was everywhere and they had some excellent hunters as part of their party, especially Drewyer. They must also have had some versatile cooks, because there were different kinds of animals and birds as they rowed along, just like the variety we get from today's markets. Each day they reported in the logs everything they shot.

Their second court martial was where the Kansas River met the Missouri. Kansas City is there now, and you can see the location from I-70. Now a Riverboat Cruise leaves from that place. The explorers arrived there on June 28th and Clark says that it is a "butifull" place for a fort, but the water is "disigreeably tasted." It doesn't take the reader of the journals very long to tell that Clark was not the best speller around. Someone said that he was an "innovative" speller. Some of his spelling seems to me to be more sensible than the correct spelling. Anyway, the men relaxed while there, but Collins and Hall did more than that. Remember Collins at St. Charles? At

Kansas City, as seen from the junction of the Kansas and Missouri Rivers

night, Collins was in charge of the whiskey, and his buddy, Hall, talked him into having a private party. When they were caught drunk the next morning, a court martial of enlisted men was ordered for 11 am. The verdict was 100 lashes for Collins and 50 for Hall. Neither Lewis nor Clark sat on the court. The sentence was carried out at 3:30 pm the same day. That kind of quick justice would be nice today. The next day they were ready to go back to work and no lawyers had to be paid.

The Corps' first Fourth of July celebration was near present day Atchison, Kansas, where the 4th of July 1804 Creek (which they named) enters the Missouri River. This is the furthest point that Glenn Bishop's replica reached when it followed the trail in 1996. At that time there was a big welcome and, in a ceremony , the name of the creek which had been called White Clay, was now restored to its original name. At this creek, as Clark wrote, "we dined on corn Captain Lewis walked on the shore above the creek and discovered a high mound from the top of which he had an extensive view." When Lena and I were on this mound, or bluff, in 1996 we saw Amelia Earhart's home, where she was raised. Learning about Lewis and Clark when she was young might have given her the adventurous spirit she had. Just north of her home is Independence Creek (which Lewis and Clark also named) and is the place where The Corps camped that night.

Both Lewis and Clark sat on the next court on July 12th because the offense was punishable by death. Willard was tried for sleeping while on sentinel duty, a breach of the

CORRECTION

The first 3 sentences after COUNCIL BLUFFS
at the bottom of page 9 and the top of page 10
have been mixed up because of a computer
glitch, and should read as follows:

The Oto and Missouri Nations finally
arrived on August 3rd and the Council Bluffs
meeting took place with long speeches by
everyone, especially Lewis, who gave the
message that Jefferson had sent to all tribes,
offering them peace and a close association
with the U.S. We visited the monument and park
that has been built there on a high bluff
overlooking the river. It is in the north end
of Council Bluffs, Iowa, and you should visit
it just to take pictures of the view.

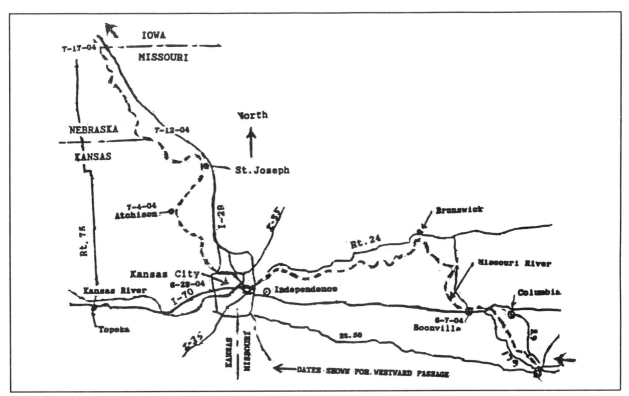

Map 3: Travel during the first summer on the outward bound portion of the expedition.

articles of war, and as Clark put it, "tending to the probable destruction of the party." He got 25 lashes on his bare back each night at sunset for 4 consecutive nights. This was near the present Kansas-Nebraska-Missouri line.

They got to the Platte River, south of present day Omaha, on July 21st, and had difficulty getting around the sand that had washed down the Platte. The captains and 6 men rowed up the Platte in the smaller boats for two miles and found the river was 900 yards wide. Clark walked on shore and saw a great many wolves.

They camped a few days near present day Omaha to try to find some Indians from the Oto or Pawnee tribes, so they could have a smoke with them and give them U.S. flags and medals, and also for Clark to catch up on his mapmaking. One man showed him a "Tumer" (abscess) on his breast on July 23rd and he (Clark) lanced it on the 26th. It discharged 1/2 pint of fluid. That was some operation to have to perform out in the wild! Today they could have got him for practicing medicine without a license.

COUNCIL BLUFFS

The Oto and Missouri Nations finally arrived on August 3rd and the Council Bluffs meeting visited the monument and park that has been built there on a high bluff overlooking the river. It is in the north end of Council Bluffs, Iowa, and you should visit it, just to take pictures of took place with long speeches by everyone, especially Lewis, who gave the message that Jefferson had sent to all tribes, wishing them peace and a close association with the U.S. We the view. There is another bluff on the Nebraska side of the river, that is probably the real council site, because the river has changed its course many times in 190 years. This is south of Blair, Nebraska near Fort Atchison State Historical Park. Why don't you visit them both and decide for yourself which is the original location? You might want to join in the vigorous discussions on the subject.

On August 7th the captains dispatched 4 men with orders to bring 2 deserters back or to shoot them. They brought Reed back on the 17th and he had to run the gauntlet four times and was excluded from the main part of the party, a disgrace. The other, a nonpermanent member got away. The Indians watched the trial and said they were satisfied with the outcome.

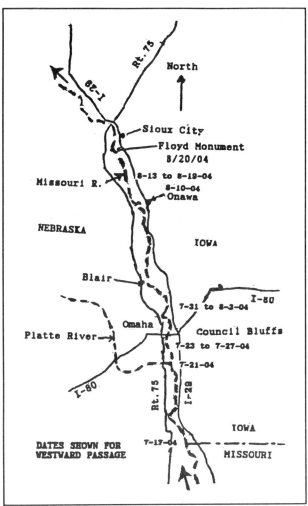

Map 4: Late summer, outward bound. Meetings with many Indian tribes in the area of Council Bluffs.

We saw the second replica of the 'barge', now referred to as the "Discovery," at the Lewis and Clark State Park in Onawa, Iowa between I-29 and the river. It was in the water of an oxbow lake which had been the Missouri River before it cut a new channel. It was alongside the replicas of the red and the white pirogues that had also been part of the Lewis and Clark 'fleet'. All three had been built in 1985-87 by a group gathered together by Ron Williams, Park Director. They were lucky to have a boat craftsman in the group, Butch Bouvier, who followed Clark's drawings as closely as possible.

In 1996 Ron was host to the Lewis and Clark Trail Heritage Foundation for a day of fun while they were staying at the Sioux City Hilton for their annual meeting. He had the barge and white pirogue sailing in a high wind down the 1-1/2 mile oxbow lake, to the excited cheers of the members. Campers can camp right on the lake at the park. A lovely

Replica of the 55 ft. "Barge" at Lewis and Clark State Park in Onawa, Iowa.

Replicas of the Red and White Pirogues at Lewis and Clark State Park in Onawa, Iowa.

campground.

Lewis and Clark camped near there on August 10, 1804 and the next morning they hiked to visit Indian King Black Bird's grave. This 'King' was one that gained power over his people because he slyly used arsenic to get rid of his opposition. He was buried on his horse so that he could have a wide view of the Missouri River below. I don't think that either the Democrats or Republicans have tried the arsenic bit yet.

Sergeant Floyd died on August 20, probably from appendicitis. They buried him on a bluff that now has a small park and a tall obelisk monument that can be seen south of Sioux City on the east side of I-29. The Corps then had an election to nominate Floyd's successor as sergeant, the honor going to Cass, and he was officially appointed on the 26th.

The Indians told the captains about a mystic hill up the White Stone River (now the Vermillion River) that had little people with big heads living there. These people had sharp arrows, and would kill anyone that came near them. All the tribes were terrified of them, and would not think of going anywhere near. This incited the captains' curiosity so they took a party of 10 men to investigate. This was about 7 miles from the Missouri and took them all day August 25th. They didn't find anything but a hill with a beautiful view of the plains. Ordway said "We saw several holes in the ground." I can't explain the reason for the superstitions of the Indians. But if we can get the extraterrestrial experts on the trail, they will find an answer to the little men with big heads. Maybe they can attribute the holes in the top of the hill to flying saucers. When the Corps was there, it was a hot day, and they were plenty weary when they got back to the river that night. They didn't meet up with the main party until the next morning. Today that hill is called Spirit Mound, and when we saw it, it was a farm, with tall corn all around it. There was an engraved sign on Highway 19 with the story of the little men and the Lewis and Clark visit. Shannon got lost on the day they returned to the boat.

Shannon, the youngest member of the party, went ashore near where Vermillion, South Dakota is now, to help Drewyer find their lost horses. He became separated from Drewyer, and unknowingly went upstream faster than the boats, thinking he was behind. After 16 days and about 170 (boat) miles, he became exhausted and starved and sat down on the bank, hoping to see a trading boat or Indians to help him. He had one horse left, and thought he might have to eat it, because his shot was gone. On September 11th the boats came by and

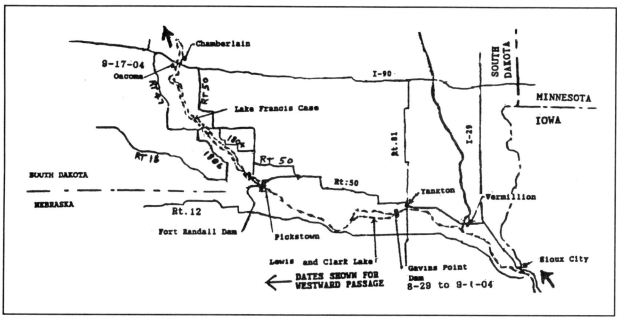

Map 5: Late summer passage up the Missouri River. (Westward Passage: Aug. 29, 1804 to Sept. 17, 1804.)

the men were overjoyed to see him and have him back. Although he took a lot of kidding about that for the rest of his life, I believe that it wasn't his fault that he became lost. During that time the Corps didn't move a mile on the last 3 days of August due to the Indian Councils near Yankton. How was he to know that? Remember, Drewyer didn't find the horses, Shannon did. He was probably so intent on finding the horses that he lost Drewyer. He got lost a year later in the Montana mountains because of another mix-up that wasn't his fault. That time they sent him up one stream to hunt while they turned around, went back down to a fork, and went up another stream. He was kidded about that too, but they were all fond of him. He survived the trip and later in life he became a respected judge in the Missouri territory.

Gavins Point Dam, the lowest one on the Missouri River, is built at Calumet Bluff, the point where Lewis and Clark's meeting with the friendly Yankton Sioux took place from

August 29th to September 1st. One of their interpreters, Dorion, arranged for the council, and now, 190 years later, the Dorion Gardens surround the Interpretive Center, which is on the bluff overlooking the entire area.

This is a worthwhile stop on the Lewis and Clark Trail, and there are many good campgrounds in the area.

Lena and I camped at Randall Dam, (the second dam going upriver), where the Corps was on September 6th, and poor Shannon probably rushed through that spot hoping to catch up with those that were behind him. Our next campground was in Chamberlain, South Dakota, across from Oacoma, where the Corps camped, and they thought it was as beautiful as we did because Lewis wrote glowingly that it was a "beatifull bowling green in fine order." He saw a grove of plum trees. We camped in a grove of plum trees. The Corps (including Shannon) was in high spirits when they were there. So were we.

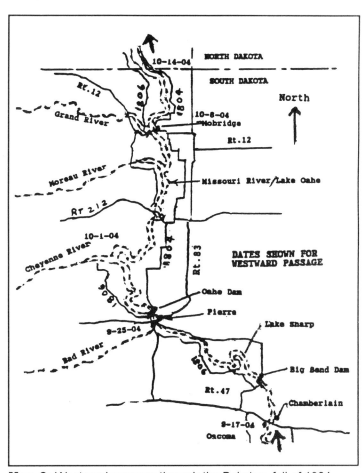

Map 6: Westward passage through the Dakotas, fall of 1804.

UNFRIENDLY SIOUX

But when they got to where Pierre, the capital of South Dakota is now, there was trouble brewing that very nearly caused the end of the expedition. The Teton Sioux nation had resolved to stop them from proceeding on up the river. When the Corps came near to the Sioux village on September 24th, they arranged for a meeting for the next day. They anchored 70 yards from shore on a sand bar, and set up a canopy on the bar for a meeting place, and the Indians arrived.

After smoking and speaking, the chiefs were invited to go on board the barge, and received 1/4 glass of whiskey apiece. Because they became troublesome, and faked drunkenness, Clark and 5 men took them to shore in one of the pirogues. At the shore, the

Indians grabbed the boat's rope and declared that Clark could not go on.

Red-haired Clark got a little hot, and drew his sword, and "spoke in verry positive terms." On board the barge, Lewis ordered all men to arms. The large swivel gun was loaded with 16 musket balls and the other two small ones were loaded with buckshot. The warriors on shore had their bows strung and arrows out of the quivers. Clark was not permitted by the Indians to return, so he sent the pirogue back to the barge, which instantly returned with 12 armed and determined men. While the chiefs counseled among themselves, Clark offered his hand in friendship, but it was refused. As Clark got into the pirogue and pushed off, the chiefs decided they wanted to go aboard the barge again and he took them in. No guns or arrows were discharged and no one was hurt. That's what I call a cliffhanger.

This incident showed that Clark knew Indians very well. If a battle had occurred there, the expedition would have had to turn back, because they never could have prevailed against thousands of natives in battle. It might have been like Custer's last stand. Then England would undoubtedly have reached the Columbia first, and Oregon and Washington, and maybe Idaho, would now be theirs. That night the corps proceeded on about a mile and stayed on what they called Bad Humored Island. The Bad River enters the Missouri from the west at about that place and today there is a campground right at the confluence.

Two more treacherous incidents occurred for the Corps in the next 5 days, requiring both a show of force and masterful diplomacy. On the 27th one of the pirogues accidentally ran into and broke the anchor rope of the barge while 3 chiefs were onboard. The captains and sergeants had to quickly shout orders to man the oars, which excited the chiefs. The chiefs hollered to their men on shore, and immediately 200 armed Indians lined the shore line.

Looking north at the Bad River near its confluence with the Missouri River, site of the Teton Sioux and Corps controversy. Ft. Pierre, South Dakota.

The barge had to run ashore to keep from being swept down river, and had to remain there overnight, while trying unsuccessfully to recover the anchor. The Corps was "much exposd to the accomplishment of their hostile intentions." In the morning a group of Indians called 'Soldiers', grabbed the boat's rope, refusing to let them proceed. The swivel guns were manned. Clark threw a carrot (a twist) of tobacco to the chief, and spoke as to 'touch his pride'. He took the fire from the port gunner. They dropped the rope. Clark had saved another day.

A heavy guard was necessary and they had little sleep until around October 1st, when they passed Teton Sioux country, about where the Cheyenne River enters the Missouri.

Just because the Pierre country was unfriendly to the explorers doesn't mean there is anything unfriendly today. Just the opposite. When we got to Pierre, we found a city park with free camping, right on the river, and it even had electric hookups free. You can't get any more friendly than that. While you are there, don't miss seeing the Verendrye Plate that French explorers left there in 1743, a long time before Lewis and Clark. No one knew where it was until three high school kids were playing up on a knoll across the river from Pierre, in Fort Pierre, in 1923, and found the lead plate. It was made for King Louis XV, and claims the land for France. There is a road up to the site, where there is now a monument, but the plate is displayed in the Museum in Pierre, where it has been taken for safekeeping.

King Louis XV claim to Louisiana. Fort Pierre, South Dakota.

Pierre is actually on the upper end of Lake Sharp, formed by Big Bend Dam, the third dam going upriver. Just above Pierre is the Oahe Dam, that forms Lake Oahe. This beautiful lake extends nearly to Bismarck, North Dakota, 231 miles, and is a boater's delight. If you plan to vacation in that country, bring your boat, for there are boat ramps everywhere, and plenty of fine campgrounds. You will enjoy visualizing how it was to paddle through that hostile country 200 years ago.

FRIENDLY INDIANS

When the Corps got to the Mobridge, South Dakota area, around October 9th, Lewis and Clark had a meeting with friendly Arikara Indians. Clark's servant, York, the only black member of the Corps, had a great time showing off his strength to the Indians, who had never seen a black man before. He had a good sense of humor, and made himself look even more horrible than Clark wished. But the fun was enjoyed by the Corps and Indians alike. The Corps shot off the air gun that they had brought along "which astonished them much." The interesting thing about the Arikara natives is that they were "not fond of Spirt Licquer of any kind." Lena and I camped at the Mobridge campground south of town, both in 1985 and in 1994, and the people there are very knowledgeable about the local Lewis and Clark history. That is a nice thing about following the Lewis and Clark Trail. The people along the way will add information about what happened to the explorers at that particular location.

On October 13th J. Newmon was court-martialed for "mutinous expression." (He probably told Lewis where to go). He got 75 lashes on the next day and was permanently banned from the Corps. The disbandment was what bothered him most, and he pleaded with Lewis to reinstate him, but he was sent back to St. Louis the next spring when the barge returned. Mutiny could not be forgiven. The Indian chiefs watched the 75 lashes and cried for him. They thought the punishment should be death, not lashing, which they thought was too extreme. Indians seldom beat their own people. They killed them occasionally, but they didn't like the idea of beatings. This happened near the present South Dakota/North Dakota line.

If you are driving north along the river in South and North Dakota I hope you notice the significance of the route numbers, which apply to the years that the Corps went up and down the river. You can follow Route 1804 on the east side much of the way, or Route 1806 on the west side. We drove the west side and saw Sitting Bull's burial site at Fort Yates, just north of the border. The Corps passed there on October 15th. (See Map 7.)

A few miles south of Interstate 94 in North Dakota, be sure to stop (and camp) at Fort Lincoln State Park, to see the museum, the reconstructed "On a Slant" Mandan Indian village, and the fort that Custer departed from, when leaving on his last campaign in 1876. Lewis and Clark passed there on October 20, 1804 and saw what was the remains of the original Indian village, which was built on a bluff overlooking the Heart River as it enters the Missouri. We camped there in 1985, 1994, and 1996 and at night we attended the hilarious play at Fort Lincoln, depicting life at the fort during the 1870's. When you buy your ticket to this play, you are given a bag of peanuts to throw at the villains when they misbehave. Believe me, you will always remember that play.

On October 21, 1804, freezing rain and snow started, and the next 60 miles until they reached the Mandans, the weather was bad. Clark had rheumatism so bad he couldn't move, and Lewis treated him with "a hot stone raped in flannel." They passed present day Bismarck and Washburn, seeing many Indians on the bank of the river who were "hallooing and singing," as Sgt. Gass wrote on the 25th. To a group of men looking for a place to spend the winter, this must have made them feel pretty good. They stopped at the Knife River (near Stanton) on October 27th.

When Lena and I were at Knife River in 1985, it was an Indian Village Historic Site. I joined a canoe trip that the park rangers conducted, one where we had to carry our canoes over the sandy places, which really brought me closer to understanding the life of the men of the Corps of Discovery.

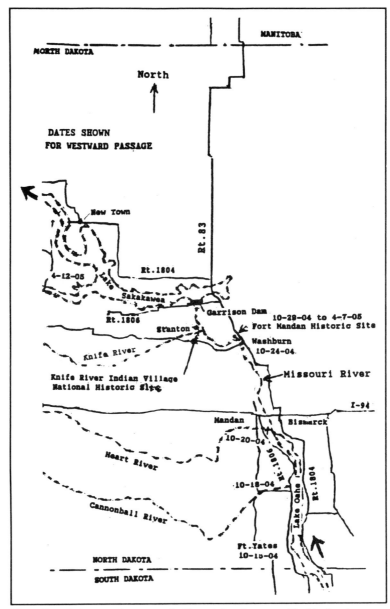

Map 7: Winter quarters were built and the Corps settled in to share the company of the Mandan Indians over the winter, from November 1804 to April 1805. See Fort Mandan Historic Site north of present day Bismarck, North Dakota.

Chapter 2

A SOCIAL WINTER
October 29, 1804 to April 7, 1805

THE PADDLING STOPS

The last river mileage entry in their journals was 4 miles on the 27th of October. Mileage entries resume again the next spring on April 7, 1805, when they again headed upriver. In between, they built Fort Mandan and spent a social winter with the Mandan and Hidatsa Indians. The boats went as far as where Stanton is now, but there were no trees which they could use to build a fort for the winter, so they went back down river a few miles to find a site for what became Fort Mandan. It was named after the friendly Indians living there. Clark found a suitable place to build on November 2nd, and by November 16th, the huts were finished enough to move in. It had two rows of 14 ft. square huts, set at what I think was about a 60 degree angle to each other, with a 56 ft. long wall to close the open side. That would leave a triangular open area inside for muster. In addition, Ordway describes a provision and smoke house that was 14x24 ft. This probably was in the angle formed at the back of the compound, a 24 ft. wall completing the back of a three-sided room. This is a guess.

Today, Fort Mandan has been rebuilt at the closest available spot, down river from the original one, which has now been washed away by the river. It now has a visitors center and campground next to it. It is near Washburn, North Dakota, about 40 miles north of Bismarck. Washburn is now building an Interpretive Center, which will make

Fort Mandan, near Washburn, North Dakota. The Corps of Discovery wintered here November 1804 to April 1805.

the Lewis and Clark Trail still more interesting.

On November 14, 1804, ice began to form on the river, and cakes that broke up occasionally flowed down, making it dangerous to use the river to get around. The trouble was that one of the pirogues was down river 30 miles, where hunters were getting supplies for winter. The Captains sent a man by horseback to find out about it. He and Drewyer came back the next day with details of the problem, so a man, probably Shields or Bratton, with

19

tin sheets to protect the front of the pirogue, and with a tow rope, was sent to the pirogue, with instructions to get back to the fort soon. That tin on the bow made the pirogue into an icebreaker. When Lewis planned this expedition the year before he thought of everything, even tin sheets for an icebreaker. But, maybe those tin sheets (probably iron or steel, because I can remember when the Model T Ford, made of steel, was called a Tin Lizzie) were cut out of cooking pans. On November 19th the pirogue arrived with 32 deer, 12 elk, and a buffalo. Quite a hunting trip!

The winter at Fort Mandan was not so bad for the explorers, even though the weather was bitter cold, and there were many frosted ears, noses, fingers, and feet. That's because they were so busy. The hunters were out frequently, the blacksmiths had all they could do to keep up with the needs of the fort, and with the Indians that brought axes, knives, etc, to be repaired. The Indians paid for the blacksmith work with corn, pumpkins, and other food.

The Indians trusted the healing methods of Lewis and Clark, so they came to the fort when their own methods failed. An Indian boy who was outdoors all night in 40 degrees below zero weather on the 9th of January with light clothing, froze his feet. His father brought him to the fort. They thought he would be all right, but on the 27th Lewis had to amputate his toes. Then he had to saw more off his toes on the 31st. On February 23rd, the father of the boy took him home in a sleigh.

The fort became a maternity ward on February 11th. Seventeen year-old Sakakawea, wife of interpreter Charbonneau, who was living at the fort, had trouble giving birth to her first baby. At Jessomme's (another interpreter's) advice, Lewis administered two rings of rattlesnake rattle, broken in small pieces and added to a glass of water, and in 10 minutes she gave birth to a son, Baptiste. This child, when about 8 weeks old, left with the explorers as they set out in their canoes on the trip to the Pacific. He eventually became an educated man and spent 6 years with the crowned heads of Europe. He became much beloved of the crew, and Clark gave him his nickname, "Pomp." (If you have visited Pompeys Pillar, on the Yellowstone River, east of Billings, you probably remember that it was named for him. Clark called it Pompy's Tower).

There were a lot of social events during the winter, both at the fort and at various villages. The Indians loved to hear Cruzat play his fiddle, with the Corp dancing. To the Indians, the Corps was like a traveling concert group. They danced at the fort and at the villages. The villagers also danced for the Corps. The Indian dances often were more earthy, very earthy, and the Corps didn't mind that a bit. Many of them ended up ON the earth. (If you want more details of those dances you will have to consult the Lewis and Clark Journals at your local library.)

Lewis's speeches to the Indians always included the protection power of the great father in Washington. The time came, on November 30th, to prove that protection, when the Sioux attacked a party of Mandan and Wetersoons and it was feared that they would attack the village. Clark and 23 men, in a hour, headed for the village and flanked it. The Indians were "supprised, and a little allarmed at the formadable appearence of my party." This action impressed the local Indians immensely. It must have impressed the enemy too, for there was no attack.

It seemed that the natives and the soldiers were becoming allies. Lewis and 15 men joined the Indians in a buffalo hunt. They got 10 buffalo and had a chance to view the way Indians killed buffalo from horseback with bow and arrows.

Lewis formed a close friendship with Black Cat, the Grand Chief of the Mandans. Lewis says "this man possesses more integrity, firmness, inteligence and perspicuety of mind than any Indian I have met with in this quarter." When we read the journals written through the winter we notice the many number of times that Black Cat brings other chiefs to visit the fort. He asked the same kind of questions about white people's way of life that they were asking about the Indians. A very intelligent man.

March 2, 1805 was a day that reminded the captains that they were in a race with the British to get to the Pacific. The competition became more serious when LaRoque of the North West Company (British) visited them from his company's establishment on the Assinniboin River with the news that McTavish, the company's leader, had died. McTavish was the one that was holding back his company from investing any more in westward expansion. Now that he was gone, North West, under MacKenzie, would try to get to the Pacific as soon as possible to claim the whole Columbia basin for England. Under this new pressure, the captains determined to head upriver just as soon as the ice in the river was gone.

Final preparations were made in March; 6 new canoes were made from cottonwood trees; Charbonneau quit to get better terms, but was hired back under the captains' terms; they caulked the barge and the pirogues. On April 1st the boats were put in the water. The 55 ft. barge was packed with scientific specimens for Jefferson. Corporal Warfington was put in charge of taking it down to St. Louis. Two pirogues and 6 canoes were packed for the upriver journey, and they all left at 4 pm on April 7, 1805. Fifteen people went down river; 31 went upriver with Lewis and Clark.

Those going upriver with Lewis and Clark wouldn't see another human being for 4 months. White men had not explored any of the land upriver from this point and what information they had was from consultations with Indians. If I had been going with them I would have been very excited, but might have had a few butterflies in my stomach.

Before you (the tourist), leave the Sakakawea Lake area, visit Garrison Dam and take a tour of the power house. They have a large mural of Sakakawea in the lobby. This dam holds back the Missouri River to form Lake Sakakawea, third largest man made reservoir in the U.S. Also, about 70 miles west there is a beautiful drive that you can take which is on Route 22 that goes over the Little Missouri River and through the Killdeer Mountains. It has a beautiful gorge.

Chapter 3

UPRIVER TO GREAT FALLS AND THE PORTAGE
April 7, 1805 to July 15, 1805

THE PADDLING STARTS AGAIN

It is impossible to now see the places that Lewis and Clark saw for the first 19 days as they headed westward, for it is now under the waters of Lake Sakakawea, which goes almost to the confluence of the Yellowstone River at the Montana border. Even so, there are a lot of places to camp on this lake today, and we camped at some of them. In 1985, 1992, and

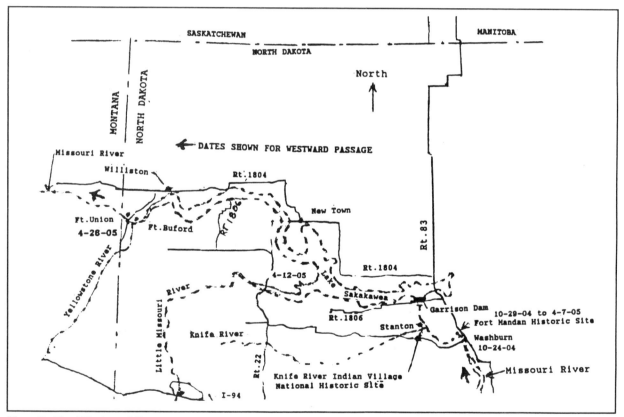

Map 8: The Westward Passage commences again in the spring of 1805.

1996 we camped at the Garrison Dam or the Lewis and Clark State Park, east of Williston, North Dakota. We wish we could have spent more time at both of these, especially if we had had our boat with us.

The Yellowstone confluence is almost to Montana, and when the Corps reached that

point, they had paddled, poled, and pulled on ropes for 275 miles, by their calculations. They had also surveyed the confluence of the Little Missouri and the White Earth rivers. When the mosquitos weren't bothering them, the blowing sand was. The fine sand even got into Lewis's pocket watch. It was in their eyes, their lungs, their water, and their food. Counting two days they stopped because of violent head winds, they still averaged 14 miles a day!

Were they discouraged at all the work and troubles that they had gone through? Heck, no! They celebrated with fiddle playing, dancing, and good humor. It must have been a pleasure to have been captain over a crew like that. Today you can visit the park at the confluence and read a large informative sign there which has direct quotes from the captains account in the journals which they wrote on April 25 & 26, 1805.

Looking south at the confluence of the Yellowstone and Missouri Rivers. The Missouri flows from left to right.

They made 114 miles the next week after leaving the confluence; when they reached what they called 2000 mile creek, because that was how far it was from the Mississippi River. This is now Poplar River in Montana, which they reached on May 3rd. The next day the rudder irons on the white pirogue broke, but those clever blacksmiths repaired them. They still made 18 miles per day from the Yellowstone River to the Milk River where they arrived on May 8, 1805. In that area the Missouri River is today pretty much like it was then, because it's still a river, not a lake.

The Fort Peck Dam is just upriver from the Milk River, and it has a campground which we have stayed in

Story on the sign at this site

Thursday and Friday, April 25 and 26, 1805:

Rich wildlife heralded the expeditions arrival at the Yellowstone / Missouri River confluence. Impatient, Lewis ascended the south bluff to view the "wide and fertile vallies." He camped Thursday night on the Yellowstone. On the winding Missouri, fierce winds nearly swamped Clark's canoes, and ice colleted on the oars. He camped on the south bank after 14 river miles.

On Friday Lewis sent Joseph Fields up the Yellowstone. He passed a well-timbered island, saw bighorn sheep, and reported "country ....like that of the Missouri." Clark's boats stopped just past the confluence. Finding them "at this long wished for spot," Lewis ordered "a dram issued to each person." A fiddle appeared and the evening was spent "with much hilarity, singing and dancing."

The captains reported "immence numbers of antelopes," "beaver in every bend," elk deer, buffalo and nesting magpies, ducks, geese, and eagles. In the bottoms grew cottonwood, oak, ash, elm, willow, and many berry bushes. Clark measured both rivers at the confluence: Missouri was 520 yards wide, (330 of it water) and the Yellowstone was 858 yards wide (297 of it water).

three different years. The reason we like that area is that it seems so remote. There is a view from a hill on the south end of the dam causeway that seemed to be ours alone, for we didn't see anyone within miles on all of our visits. And if you look at the map you won't see any roads alongside and parallel to the river that tend to civilize the area from there to Fort Benton. That is 412 river miles, according to the Journals. Where else in the country today, is it so remote for so far?

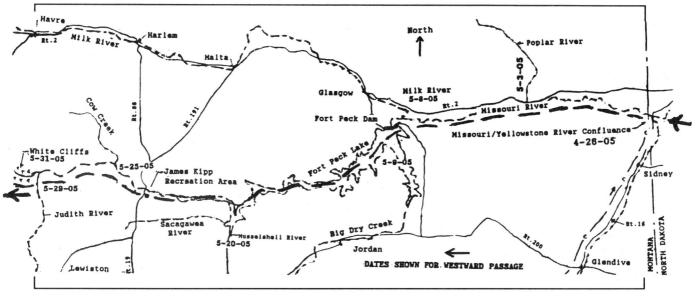

Map 9: Spring months on the Westward Passage through present day eastern Montana.

May 14th was a tough day for the corps, both on land and on the river. Six men went out to kill a large bear, but, even with bullets in it, it attacked and almost got some of them. They all scattered like chickens in a barnyard, two into a canoe and two jumping into the river over a 20 ft. bank with the bear right behind them. The others hid in the willows while they reloaded. The bear always attacked the one who had just fired, so there must have been some excitement for awhile until a bullet to the brain finally ended the fray. I'll bet there was some laughing (at themselves) around the campfire that night.

The second incident that happened that day was similar to what happened a month before at the mouth of the Little Missouri River. Timid Charbonneau was at the helm of the white pirogue again, and it upset again. Drewyer saved the day on April 13th, and Cruzat saved it this time by threatening to shoot him if he didn't turn the rudder correctly. Sakakawea also helped, by leaning over and retrieving floating articles. The captains were on shore, and were relieved when Cruzat and two others got the water filled boat ashore.

After such a tough day the captains issued a gill of spirits to everyone.

I hope the reader does not become as confused about the spelling of Sakakawea (Birdwoman) as I was as we traveled along the Trail. In North Dakota the word is spelled like Lake Sakakawea. As you drive into Montana you will note that the signs spell the word Sacagawea. Then as you proceed over the mountains into Idaho the signs spell it Sacajawea. I have used all three spellings, depending on the location of the story being told.

They passed the Musselshell River on the 20th and got to present James Kipp State Park on the 23rd. This part of the river can be reached today via a 60 mile road (Route 191) from Malta, Montana which is on Highway 2. We went down this road in 1996 and parked illegally on the bridge over the Missouri for a moment to take pictures of the beautiful cliffs. After the first picture, the mosquitos had zeroed in

Coal Bank Landing, Virgelle, Montana. These rafters will see the White Cliffs. Lena's new fetching friend will go down river too.

on me. With a swarm around me, I snapped the second picture and started running for the van, jumped in, and took off. Parking Maids couldn't have got me off the bridge any sooner.

The Bureau of Land Management has prepared a detailed map with contour lines of the river from this point, Kipp Park, to Fort Benton, a distance of 149 river miles. They call it a Floaters Guide, and it is a boon to those taking raft trips down the river. It gives the location of every campsite of the Lewis and Clark expedition, and the site of the crossing of Chief Joseph and the Nez Perce Indians 72 years later. The Nez Perce were trying, unsuccessfully, to escape federal troops and were on their way to Canada to meet with Chief Sitting Bull. It was also in this area that Lewis (May 31st) wrote so well about the unique geology of the White Cliffs which are so well known today. If you would like to see and hear a video of Lewis's description of the White Cliffs, ask one of the well informed rangers at the museum in Fort Benton. When I was there and showed my interest in the Lewis and Clark expedition, they ran the tape for me in a nice quiet adjoining room. They probably will for you, and you will be impressed. Some day I hope to take a raft trip down the river past the White Cliffs so I can admire their beauty.

26

WHICH WAY ?

The Corps reached the fork of two large rivers on June 2nd, and they didn't know if the falls they sought were up the right or left fork. This problem held them up for the next 10 days. Which was the Missouri? They measured both, to see if the size could give them a clue. Clark took a party up the south fork for two days. Lewis's party went for four days up the north fork. On June 9th, the two captains decided that the south fork was the Missouri and named the north one Maria's River. (Now called Marias River.) The others all thought the correct fork was the north one, partly because Cruzat thought so, and he was a respected river man. But they were happy to follow the captains, in whom they had faith. They then made a cache at the forks, left all surplus equipment in it, hid the red pirogue, and left it there. That gave seven hands that had been on the pirogue to strengthen the other boats. Lewis and 4 men started walking up the north side of the south fork on June 12th and the remainder, under Clark, started paddling up the same fork the next day.

Looking east as the Marias River enters the Missouri River.

Route 87, N.E. of Fort Benton, today goes within 2 miles of the confluence of the Marias and Missouri, and you can walk up a bluff near Loma, and see the whole confluence area easily, where the explorers had such a tough decision. There are interpretive signs up there that explain the Lewis and Clark history and later explorations at this confluence. To me it seemed easy to tell that the Missouri was by far the largest of the two, but that shows how much easier hindsight is than foresight.

At this point I must tell you about the air gun that Sheilds repaired on June 10th, as they prepared to proceed on up the river. It needed a new spring, so he made one and installed it while out there on the bank of the river. I saw the remarkable gun at a meeting of the Lewis and Clark Trail Heritage Foundation in Charlottesville, Virginia in August 1995. It was near Lewis's mother's grave site that the Curator of the Virginia Military Institute showed it to us. He brought it from the institute's museum especially to show to our Foundation. It was the actual gun that Lewis bought before the trip and which the Indians were excited about and called Big Medicine. The shoulder piece of the gun was actually a tank which held the pressure of 650 psi which made the gun so deadly. It screwed into a pump for pressurizing, and (with the same thread) into the firing mechanism for firing. The actual gun was on a table in front of us but was not to be touched. However a similar gun, disassembled, was there for our examination. The air pump that created the pressure was there too. It had what was essentially a giant lag screw on one end that could be screwed into a tree, and when the shoulder air chamber was screwed into the other end it became easy to pump up the large pressures. A most ingenious gun that could fire 40 shots on a single pressurizing, the first 20 very deadly. This remarkable gun gave the Corps of Discovery a lot of respect from the Indians.

Soon after proceeding on, the Corps passed the spot where Fort Benton is today. Many tourists find that city one of the most interesting on the whole Lewis and Clark Trail. Today, the riverfront, with its signs, plaques, statues, museums, and old buildings, get you to relive the old west as few other places can. There is an old bridge crossing the Missouri River right at the city waterfront which is declared unsafe for traffic, but is used by the community for picnics, Sunday school classes, and similar functions. You can stand on the bridge and visualize how it was for the men in 6 dugout canoes and a white pirogue that passed that point, not knowing what was ahead. They were hoping that they were on the correct river, that was supposed to have some large falls no white man had ever seen. Also you can stand there and realize that 3485 miles downstream was the Gulf of Mexico, and that this was the end of the line, for passenger or freight traffic in the years after the explorers. Fort Benton, therefore, became the hub for development of that part of the west. There is a nice campground a few blocks from the waterfront.

The next 54 river miles were not easy for the Corps of Discovery. The river was getting more difficult to ascend, because of the more rapid current. The men had toothaches, tumors, and one had a fever. Many came close to being bitten by rattlesnakes on the steep river banks. How could they watch for rattlesnakes when they were pulling on those ropes?

Sacagawea (different spelling in Montana) had been sick since June 10th, 2 days before they left the forks. Clark had her moved to the rear of the pirogue under shelter so that she would be more comfortable. He bled her and gave her a dose of salts, but she wasn't getting any better. The whole party felt as Lewis did when he wrote, "This gave me some concern as well for the poor object herself, then with a young child in her arms, as from the consideration of her being our only dependence for a friendly negociation with the Snake Indians on whom we depend for horses to assist us in our portage from the Missouri to the columbia river." He gave her 2 doses of barks, opium, and laudanum. He had sulphur water brought from what is now known as Sacagawea Spring for her to drink. He believed that her disorder was from "an obstruction of the mensis in cosequence of taking could." After this treatment her pulse and her nervous symptoms improved, and she felt much freer from pain. She continued improving and was able to walk the portage route by June 28th.

PORTAGE AROUND GREAT FALLS

Lewis, who was traveling ahead on foot, saw the great falls from the north side on June 13th, and dispatched Joe Fields the next morning with a letter to Clark, who was with the boats, about the discovery. Nothing was written in the diaries about the effect this word had on the respect the men had for their two captains. They had taken the right river! Only the captains had been correct. The men must have gained new admiration for these two intelligent leaders.

Missouri River, looking west. City of Great Falls, Montana in the background. Walking path built on old railroad bed.

From Lewis's writings the falls must have been beautiful, but today there are several dams and power plants which cover up the beauty. However, the lakes that are a result make a pretty setting for the City of Great Falls, Montana. An island on one of the lakes, is now called Sacagawea Island. There is a road along the edge of the south side of the river, with signs describing the scenery, and giving quotes from the writings of Lewis and Clark.

The portage around the great falls took from June 16th, when they got to the portage

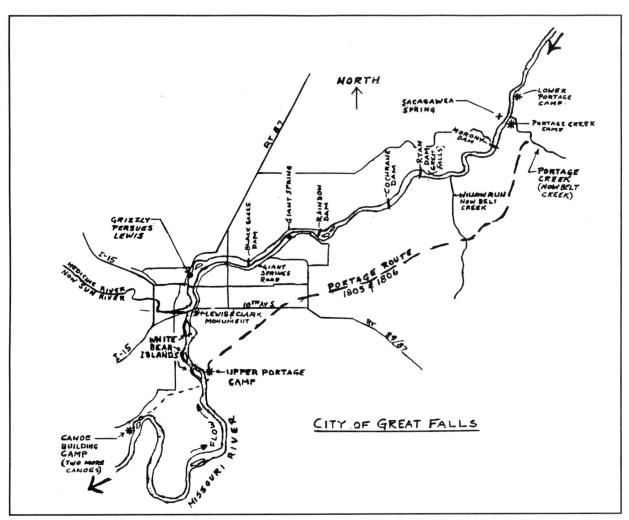

Map 10: The route of the portage around the series of water falls in the vicinity of Great Falls, Montana.

camp, until July 2nd, when the last of the canoes and baggage reached the White Bear Islands. The cliffs at the lower end of the portage were 170 ft. high and there was an additional slow rise of 250 ft. to the plain above. They found a large stream (now Belt Creek) above the next set of rapids, which was suitable for getting the boats out. They unloaded the boats at the lower point on the river, called Lower Portage Camp. (See Map 10). They then hauled the empty boats up the rapids to the stream. They could then get the boats to the plain above easier, and could carry the lighter baggage up from the lower point. They couldn't camp at the stream, because there was no wood for the fires, or for building the wagons. The whole portage was a logistical nightmare, but with the collective brains of the party they did well. After the canoes had been brought to the plain, it took about a day to travel each way between lower and upper camps. The white pirogue was not portaged, they hid it a mile below the creek.

It took until June 22nd to lay out the portage route and to build the wagons. The wagon

30

wheels were made from a 22 inch diameter cottonwood, the very largest tree they could find. The axles were made from the mast of the white pirogue.

The Lower Camp area can be seen today by the tourist but requires some hiking, and is on private land. A map of the whole portage route is available at the Lewis and Clark visitors center on the Giant Springs road in Great Falls. The Giant Springs was called 'the fountain' by Lewis and Clark, and is now a park right next to the river, and the water flowing from it is called the 'worlds shortest river'. There is also a fish hatchery there that we were free to walk through.

The first portage trip they attempted was with one canoe, and all the parts and equipment necessary to build the iron ribbed boat. Lewis had brought this unassembled boat to carry the baggage which had been in the white pirogue. Lewis stayed at the upper camp of the portage during the next 22 days with Sgt. Gass, Joseph Fields, and John Shields, who were craftsmen, doing their best to put the boat together for the next leg of their journey. They assembled it, but were unsuccessful at getting it waterproof. They had to take it apart and deposit the frame in a cache. It was a bitter disappointment for Lewis.

The next two portage trips brought 4 more canoes to the upper camp in 4 days, but the one last load with the remaining sixth canoe and baggage took 5 days. On this trip they got to Willow Run the first night, but heavy rain kept them from crossing it the next morning. So Clark took a party to the falls to get some more measurements, and to let those who wished, to see the falls and the Giant Spring. When they got near the river, a terrible storm hit them, with large hail and heavy rain. Clark, Charbonneau, and Sacagawea took refuge in a ravine under a shelving rock. The ravine, which had almost no water in it at first, rose to 15 ft. deep, with a torrent that was "turouble to behold," which took mud and large rocks with it. Charbonneau got out first, but was so petrified that he lost his gun, shot pouch, horn, tomahawk, and Lewis's wiping rod. He was too scared to even help his wife and child get out. Clark had to push Sacagawea ahead of him while he had his rifle in his other hand and was up to his waist in water. The baby had been stripped naked by the storm, and was cold. They ran fast back to the baggage to get something to cover the baby. Sacagawea was cold and was recovering from her long illness. York, who was hunting nearby, thought Clark and party had been washed into the Missouri River and over the falls. It's a miracle that they escaped.

The men that were on the plain carrying baggage were hit on their bare heads in that same hailstorm. They were left bruised and bloody. Clark lost a very valuable compass in the torrent. He thought it was gone, but two men found it the next day in the mud and rocks. That compass is now in the Smithsonian Institute, and their officials brought it to the University of Virginia in 1995, to show the members of the Lewis and Clark Trail Heritage Foundation, who were having their annual meeting there in Charlottesville.

Clark's party had to stay at Willow Creek 2 more nights to recover from the beating they got from the hail and to wait for the water in the creek to go down. Even then they had to carry the baggage across on their backs through 3 ft. of water. They arrived at the upper camp on July 1st with most of the baggage and all were anxious to proceed onward. But the metal boat was still not ready, because they could not find any pine trees for pitch to waterproof it. They tried substitutes but nothing would work. It wouldn't be declared a failure until July 9th. Lewis had planned this project two years before, in Harpers Ferry, Virginia and figured it would help in any portaging operation. It would have been a good idea if there had been pine trees in the area. He had named the boat "Experiment," and that's all it was. They decided they had to build more canoes to carry their baggage.

There are a group of 9 organizations in Great Falls that support a Lewis and Clark Fiesta each year, to commemorate this portage. It has boat rides, hikes, car tours, cookouts, and best of all, an Encampment. If you want to see Lewis or Clark, meet them at the Encampment. Perhaps you would like to meet and talk to Sacagawea and her husband, ol' Charbonneau. Or Shannon and Sheilds. Or the sergeants, or any of the Corps of Discovery. They are all at the Encampment every year. However, I tried to find Drewyer, (Drouillard) but as usual, they said he was out hunting. Of course! The year WAS 1805 and they had just completed the portage, and knew nothing of the future of the expedition. If you asked them about any of their experiences west of there, they wouldn't know what you were talking about. But there didn't seem to be anything they didn't know about what had gone on before that date, even in the personal life of the explorer whose part they played. Visit them some year, around the end of June, and join in the fun.

Clark and 7 men walked 8 miles to where suitable cottonwoods for two canoes grew, and established the canoe camp. At the same time, 4 loaded canoes struck out for the same camp, (23 river miles). By July 15th, the canoes were made, and all eight fully loaded canoes were on their way upriver again.

I thought this canoe camp location would be hard to find, but Lena and I were in for a surprise when we went looking for it in July, 1996. The washboards on the road upriver from Great Falls were terrible, so I was just crawling, to keep the dishes in the van cabinet from singing too loud a song. When a car approached from the rear I pulled way over and stopped so he could go on by. But the driver, John Cameron, stopped and asked if he could help me find something. I sheepishly told him that I was looking for the Lewis and Clark canoe camp of 190 years ago. When he answered that he owned the land that the canoe camp was on, I thought he was putting me on, but he was serious. He said that a national TV company made a film on his land with actors taking the part of the Corps of Discovery. He led me to his place and was a friendly host, letting me take pictures anywhere I wanted. I asked if the location was about 8 miles by road and 23 miles by river from White Bear Island. He figured awhile, and then answered "Yes, just about," and wondered how I got such incredible information. I told him I read it in the Lewis and Clark Journals!

Chapter 4

LOOKING FOR INDIANS WITH HORSES
July 15, 1805 to August 31, 1805

GATES OF THE MOUNTAINS

Every present day traveler should afford themselves the pleasure of the 2 or 3 hour boat trip through the 'Gates of the Mountains' which the Corps of Discovery went through on July 19, 1805. You surely won't have to paddle like they did, for the present day boat that carries a few dozen passengers is powered, and very comfortable. We saw a goat halfway up the 1200 ft. high vertical cliffs. It seemed as though it was glued up there by some giant hand. It ignored us little people down in the boats.

Lewis was with the boats as the party went through the 'gates'. Clark was walking on shore at the time and probably never saw them; he was off looking for Indians with horses. It was after dark as the boats entered and they needed a place to stay overnight. They found the only place that existed, which was on the left side about halfway through the 5 1/2 mile 'gates. This place is now called Meriwether Park, and our tour boat stopped about fifteen minutes to let us go ashore to investigate. It looked to me as if this break in the cliffs had been formed by a landslide where a section of the cliff just crumbled and fell into the river. A good geologist would have a much more professional explanation. I don't see how the Corps could have got

A mountain goat relaxing on a cliff, Gates of the Mountains.

much sleep, though, because they reached the camp after dark and at 6 am they had already got up, were back in the boats and were emerging from the 'Gates'. Lewis said that was where the "hills retreated from the river and the valley became wider."

THREE FORKS OF THE MISSOURI

Clark, who was walking ahead with 3 others, got to the Three Forks on July 25, and didn't expect Lewis and the boats to arrive for a couple days. So he kept going up the Southwest

Fork, which seemed to him the best one to find Indians. Indians were their main objective at this time. The river was getting smaller all the time and would soon run out. They knew they couldn't proceed over the mountain without horses, and Indians usually had lots of them. Sacagawea could confirm that fact about the Shoshones. So Clark, Reuben Fields and Frazier hiked up the river to the top of a mountain where they could see far ahead. Clark got heated and very thirsty. So, at the bottom of the hill he drank too much from a very cold spring and got sick. Even so, he forded the Southwest Fork (now the Jefferson River), even saving Charbonneau who was almost washed away.

Lewis made a survey of the Three Forks area from this prominent height above the Gallatin River. Notice the tour train at the bottom of the mountain.

But he got sicker, with high fever, and by the time Lewis and the rest of the Corps arrived there at the three forks, his indisposition caused Lewis to decide to rest there a couple days. Clark was probably sick that long, from something other than cold water. Lewis had a bower built to make Clark more comfortable, and treated him with medicine as any doctor would. He was okay in a few days and on July 30th they proceeded on.

At this Three Forks camp they named the three rivers; the West Fork became the Jefferson, the Middle Fork the Madison, and the East the Gallatin. Those names

---

Story on the sign at the THREE FORKS OF THE MISSOURI

This region was alive with beaver, otter, and game before the white man came. It was disputed hunting territory with the Indian tribes. Sacajawea, the Shoshone who guided portions of the Lewis and Clark Expedition, was captured near here when a child during a battle between her people and the Minnetarees. Her memories of this country were invaluable to the explorers. The Expedition, westward bound, encamped near here for a few days in the latter part of July, 1805. The following year Captain Clark and party came back, July 13, 1806 on their way to explore the Yellowstone River.

In 1808 John Colter, discoverer of Yellowstone Park, and former member of the Lewis and Clark Expedition, was trapping on a stream in this vicinity when captured by a band of Blackfeet. His only companion was killed. Colter was stripped, given a head start, and ordered to run across the flat which was covered with prickly pear. The Indians were hot on his heels, but Colter undoubtedly made an all time record that day for sprints as well as distance events. He outran the Indians over a six mile course and gained the cover of the timber along the Jefferson River. Once in the stream he dove and came up under a jam of driftwood. This hide out saved him from a lot of disappointed and mystified Indians. When night came he headed east, weaponless, and outnuding the nudists. He traveled in this condition for seven days to Fort Lisa, his headquarters at the mouth of the Big Horn River.

In 1810 the Missouri Fur Co. built a fur trading post close by, but due to the hostility of the Blackfeet Indians were forced to abandon it that fall.

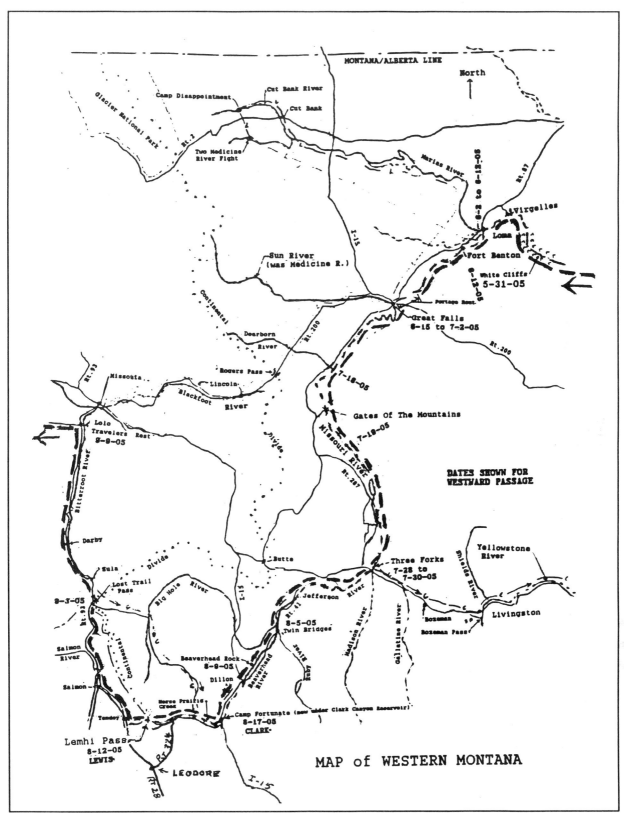

Map 11: Route of the Corps of Discovery, westbound, through western Montana (May through July of 1805).

were for the president and his cabinet and have never been changed since. The camp was at the same location as the place where Sacagawea and the Shoshones were encamped 4 or 5 years earlier, when the Minnatarees appeared and eventually killed or captured many of the Shoshones. Sacagawea was one of the captured, and was taken east to the Minnitaree (Hidatsa) village near the Mandans. That is where interpreter Charbonneau, collector of Indian wives, purchased her. She recognized this Three Forks site, remembered details of the area, and from then on she could tell the captains that they were getting closer to her people.

Three Forks is an interesting place. It is now called the Missouri Headwaters State Park and has campgrounds, an abandoned village, and an interpretive building loaded with charts and signs. From the knoll in back you can see all the rivers, and can look across to the mountain that Lewis climbed to survey, and make maps of the area. You can stroll down to see where all three rivers join to form the mighty Missouri River. While we were there in 1996 a bus pulled in, full of tourists that came from a railroad train tour of the Lewis and Clark Trail. The bus brought them from the train. Harry Fritz of the Lewis and Clark Trail Heritage Foundation was their guide, and while there, their train pulled by slowly so they could wave to it from the same knoll. I tell this to show how some people get to see the Trail; by train.

The existing town of Three Forks is south of there, where there is a Museum that is staffed by informative and very friendly people. If you like to see old stuff, that place is for you. There is an old railroad hotel there too that they have just put a lot of money into updating, that you might try if you don't have a camper. Campers that need hook-ups can stay in two modern campgrounds in the area that we have tried in 1982, '92. and '96.

UP THE JEFFERSON RIVER

Montana Route 41 follows close to the Jefferson River southward on the way up to Dillon, Montana. You can see the river getting smaller each mile, and wonder how the Corps made it through the bushes that lined the bank. They couldn't walk ashore and tow the boats through the swift water because there were too many bushes, but had to wade in the cold water along the shore. The river is so crooked that it took three miles of towing to accomplish 1 mile in a straight line. Lewis, walking ashore for awhile, tried to get back to the boats, but the brush was so thick he had to sleep ashore alone with no blankets. He contacted them the next day. It is a picturesque valley and I hope they appreciated the scenery as much as we tourists do today.

Everything went wrong on August 5th when they got to the Wisdom, (now Big Hole River at Twin Bridges, Mt.). Lewis and party, (Charbonneau, Drewyer and Gass) had been walking ahead, looking for Indians and investigating each stream that entered the Jefferson to see which way the boats should go. When he got to the Wisdom, which came in from the right, he went up it some distance and decided it was impassable. He left a note to Clark, telling him that the middle fork, now the Beaverhead River, (the left fork is now Ruby River) was the way to go. He placed the note on a green willow bush at the forks. After he left, a beaver, (they like green willow bushes), cut it down and dragged it away, the note with it. When Clark and the boats arrived, the Wisdom looked like the best way to go, so they did. After proceeding one mile, sometimes through willows that had to be cut, they stopped for the night. After a bad night on wet ground, they proceeded on until Drewyer caught up to them and told them they were on the wrong river. As they turned around to go back down river one canoe overturned and another one filled with water. Whitehouse had been thrown out of a canoe and was injured as it passed over him in the rough water. A medicine box, shot pouch, and other articles were lost. All this time Clark was suffering from a tumor on his ankle, and the men were sore and worn out. Shannon had been sent hunting up the Wisdom River and was expecting the canoes to meet him up that river, not knowing that they had turned around. In spite of all these troubles they only rested a half day on August 7th and were off again, this time up the middle fork, leaving Shannon up the other one.

Sacagawea soon noticed a large rock that she called the Beaver Head Rock ahead, and said that it was not very far from the summer retreat of her people.(Beaverhead Rock is right on Route 41 today.) This information from Sacagawea made Lewis think again about horses, so after Shannon found his way back to the Corps on the 9th, he left, on foot, with Drewyer, Sheilds, and McNeal, for a trip ahead to find her people, the Shoshones.

Clark continued with the boats for the next eight days, averaging about six miles per day, (18 river miles) until they were a few miles below the fork of what is now Horse Prairie Creek. Those eight days were very difficult, and nerves were on edge. Colter struck his wife, [CHARBONNEAU] and was severely reprimanded by Clark for doing so. The men were ready to give up. Clark had to pacify them, and somehow give them encouragement. He knew they couldn't go much further, but he knew there wasn't anything else they could do until Lewis showed up with horses. The only consolation that the men had was, that with each stroke of the oar, or each tug on the rope, they were getting closer to the top of the mountains, and I'll bet Clark used that fact to keep them going.

South of Dillon, Interstate 15 follows the river for 20 miles, and as you drive you can see the terrain that they had to pull the boats through. Lewis and Clark referred to this part of the river as the Jefferson, but above the Big Hole River forks it is now the Beaverhead. There is an I-15 exit at Barretts Dam where you will see a nice picnic ground on the other side of the river, with a pretty walking bridge that leads to it. Some RV's stay overnight in the parking lot next to the road. Signs say that a high cliff there was the place that Clark called Rattlesnake Mountain because he was almost bitten by one there. A local resident of nearby

Dillon, Larry Rose, told me that Clark was lucky, for even today there are several snake dens there.

LEWIS SCOUTS TO FIND INDIANS

Meanwhile, Lewis, Drewyer, Sheilds, and McNeal, had been moving fast since they left the crew on the 9th. They found an Indian road and covered 16 miles on the first day. They reached a junction of two creeks on the next day, and horse trails went up each fork. After surveying the creeks that flowed into the main river, Lewis concluded that the boats could go no further, and wrote a note to Clark advising him to wait here for his return, He left the note at the junction of the two creeks, (now called Clarks Canyon) and headed with his party up the west fork, which is now called Horse Prairie Creek.

On August 11th they saw their first Indian. He was on horseback, and he stopped to let Lewis get close to him, but when he saw Drewyer and Sheilds flanking him, he left in a hurry. Lewis said " I now felt quite as much mortification and disappointment as I had pleasure and expectation at the first sight of this Indian."

The next day the four men reached the upper waters of the Missouri River (a tributary of Horse Prairie Creek) and McNeal straddled the stream, and thanked God he lived long enough to bestride the endless Missouri. Then they went over the hill (Lemhi Pass) and drank from the waters of the "great Columbia River."

Signs along the trail explain the activities of the expedition.

On the 13th, Lewis saw two women, a man, and dogs near what is now the Lemhi River, but they ran away, too. Next they saw an old woman, a girl, and a child, and they came upon them so quick and so close before they saw each other that there wasn't time for the old woman to run. She just sat there, head bowed, waiting to be killed by Lewis. He took her hand and raised her up, gave her gifts and showed her he was a white man, not one of her enemies that she feared. He gave her gifts and got her to call the girl who had run away to come back to her. Lewis asked her to conduct him to her village, and they had gone 2 miles when 60 fierce warriors in battle dress galloped toward them. The old lady and girl stopped them and told them who the strangers were. The chief then welcomed them, smoked with them, and Lewis conversed with them through Drewyer who knew sign language. They were conducted to the village for more ceremonies and the presentation of the flag.

The Shoshones were hungry. The antelope in their country were much harder to kill from horseback than buffalo are, because they run faster. The only way they could get close enough to hit them with arrows was to chase them constantly, using fresh horses alternately until the antelope were worn out. This took sometimes 40 or 50 hunters. Lewis went with them one day, but 20 hunters shot nothing. Drewyer, Sheilds, and McNeal were unsuccessful too. Lewis got McNeal to make a paste from the little flour that they had left and added berries to it to make a decent meal. The next morning the same mixture was made with half of all the flour they had left and McNeal cooked it into a pudding for the four men. Some was given to the chief who thought it was good.

Lewis's problem was how to get the chief (Cameahwait) to accompany him when he returned to the Jefferson (now Beaverhead) River forks to meet Clark, and to have enough horses to carry the baggage over the mountains. When the Indians found out that there were more white men coming up the river, they thought they were being forced into a trap, and that these white men were helping their enemies. It took a lot of conversations with Cameahwait for Lewis to allay the Indian's fear and to get him to accompany them with men and horses back to meet Clark and the boats. It took him until noon on August 15th to persuade them to go, and finally first six, then a dozen more and then most of the village were on their way.

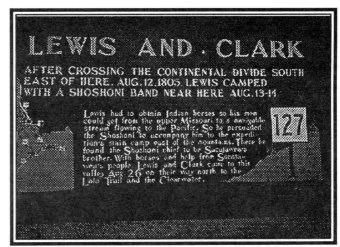

A sign near the Lemhi Pass tells of the encounter with the Shoshoni Indians, Sacajawea's tribe.

That night at the first camp, the hunters had been unsuccessful in killing any meat, so they divided the last pound of flour into six portions and finished it. The next morning the hunters were sent out, and the Indians were requested to stay away from them so as not to warn the deer. This request made the Indians suspicious of the whites again, and they sent out spies to watch the hunters. When one of the spies rode back to camp at a gallop, everyone was apprehensive. When he announced that a white (Drewyer) had shot a deer, all raced to see it. When Lewis arrived he was disgusted at the way the ravenous Indians were eating it. There wasn't any part they didn't eat. The raw intestines were a delicacy to them. If you wish to read the details of this gory orgy you will have to read the Journals, for Lewis described it very plainly.

CAMP FORTUNATE

Drewyer killed two more deer that day and everyone got their fill and were in good humor. But, as they drew closer to the forks it became plain that Clark and the boats were not waiting for them there. The note that Lewis had left on August 10th was still there. Cameahwait again became suspicious and took another precaution to guard against an ambush. He disguised the whites as Indians; which Lewis complied with and even put his cocked hat on Cameahwait to gain more of his trust. The Indians were all tense, as if waiting for the battle to begin. While all stood there at the forks waiting, Drewyer (Cameahwait had dressed him like an Indian) and an Indian went down river on the morning of August 17th to locate the boats, which they did in a short time.

The emotional scene that followed, as the whites came up and intermingled with the Indians, must have been as joyful as any has been before or since. Drewyer reached Clark early, and when Sacagawea saw the Indians, she signaled to Clark that they were her people. The girl that had been with her when she was captured five years before was there, and they went crazy to see each other. When Sacagawea came up to Lewis and Cameahwait's camp, she recognized the chief as her brother, and there was more jubilation. The Indians danced and sang and the Corps of Discovery must have been so very glad to see horses. They knew that the boat dragging was over.

Sacagawea was then used as the interpreter that she had been carried up the river to be. Before her arrival, communication had been by signs only. Now the real negotiation for horses began. The captains told the Indians that they would need as many horses as

Campground at Clark Canyon Reservoir. Camp Fortunate, where Sacagawea met Cameahwait, is now underwater.

the Indians could spare, and would buy them if they could not find a way to go down the local river to the Columbia. They only bought three at that time and Clark got two of them to leave the next morning on his way over the divide.

UP ROUTE 324 IN 1992

The location of this important meeting, called Camp Fortunate, was where Clark Canyon Reservoir is located today. There is a public campground on the shore of the reservoir. There

Lemhi Pass, looking west over the continental divide into Idaho.

are toilets there, but no other services. That is all right because there are no camping charges either. Highway 324 leaves I-15 there, and passes Cameahwait Park (named for Sacajawea's brother) and a bridge over Horse Prairie Creek before it follows the creek westward. It is a slowly rising road that leads over the divide at Bannock Pass (Elev. 7681), and the driving is slow to avoid hitting cattle that lay down in the road. The Lemhi Pass road was what we were looking for, and is a right turn off Route 324.

When we saw a signpost on the right saying 'Lemhi Pass', at what looked to us like a driveway, we didn't believe it could be correct, (we should have) so we proceeded on over Bannock Pass and down to the town of Leadore, Idaho on the Lemhi River. We had missed Lemhi Pass, and that is unforgivable for anyone following the Lewis and Clark Trail. I am including these details so campers following the trail do not do the same thing.

We thought maybe we could go over the pass from the west side, so we drove to Tendoy, Idaho and asked about the road at the local store/post office. When the lady heard that I wanted to go over the pass that Lewis and Clark took, she wanted to know all about what kind of a vehicle I was driving. When she heard we had a two wheel drive, 1 ton van, with a pop top that was in its lowered position, she had her doubts, but she said that maybe we could make it, because she knew of a local man that had made it that day. I wanted to go up there pretty bad, and since Lena has more courage than I have, and she said "Lets go," we started out.

The road was paved for a few miles and then became a not too bad dirt road. Then when we started the last steep, maybe two mile ascent, that gained what might be 1500 ft. with a steep drop on our right, and only two ruts, that scared feeling in my spine made me wonder if I was having fun. The worst part was, that at the steepest part, the ruts made the van lean outward instead of inward. The Lemhi Pass was mighty deserted when Lena and

I went over it that day on June 30, 1992. There is a good view both east and west from the summit, which is 7373 ft. elevation. It seemed as though we could see both the Atlantic and Pacific Oceans! Sacajawea Historical Park is on the east side of the summit in a nice little grove. There are two or three tables and a dedication plaque, but that is about all. Very private. We were the only ones there, and there was news on the radio that they expected snow in the region. If it wasn't for that we would have stayed all night.

It was evening and we thought about going down the east side but we thought that road might be even worse, so back down that west side we went. I have always had the practice of shifting to low gear when going down a steep hill. Not that hill, with the precipice on one side. Low gear was too fast. If I had turned off the engine while it was in low gear, it might have been slow enough, but I wouldn't have any power brakes. We worried about what would happen if another vehicle was on the way up at the same time. If that had happened, the other guy might have backed down to a hairpin turn and we could have passed, but I surely couldn't have backed up the steep grade and stayed in the ruts. I guess we were all alone on the mountain all the time we were on it, so we got down okay. Then we found a nice campground at Salmon, Idaho.

CLARK TO EXPLORE SALMON RIVER

On August 18th Lewis had his 31st birthday at Camp Fortunate, and he worried that he had as yet done but little to further the happiness of the human race and resolved to redouble his exertions in the future. He resolved "to live for mankind, as I have heretofore lived for myself." That sounded to me like a pretty good attitude to take hold of the world today. After Clark, 11 men, Charbonneau, and Sacajawea left Camp Fortunate to go over the mountain to the Shoshone village, Lewis had the rest of the men make pack saddles, so they could carry all their baggage on horses when Clark's party hopefully returned with them. He also made medicine from the plant species that he had collected. (Can you imagine a Captain in the army today being able to make medicine for the men from the plants he had collected?) He had a cache made for the articles that they would not need on the trek westward and had the canoes sunk in a pond near the forks and weighted them down with rocks.

Clark and party reached the Shoshone village on August 20th, had a ceremony, and questioned Cameahwait about the terrain westward and whether there was navigation possible on any of the rivers. He said they were all impassable, and that the only way the Nez Perce Indians could get over the mountains was far to the north. Clark agreed on the northern route, but first had to make his own survey to be sure. So he set out that same day, going down the Lemhi and Salmon Rivers with his party and an Indian guide. Sacajawea and

Charbonneau were left at the village to accompany the Indians to Lewis's camp the next day with horses.

While Clark was going down the Lemhi and Salmon Rivers in Idaho, Sacajawea, with her husband, brother, and 50 Indians and horses, arrived at Lewis's camp as promised. The baggage was loaded on the borrowed horses and on the 24th they proceeded on. It is interesting to note what Lewis wrote about one Indian woman that had been leading two of the pack horses along the trail. When she stopped and let the horses go on ahead, Lewis asked Cameahwait what was the matter. The answer was that she was falling back to have a baby, and would be along soon. In about an hour she showed up with a baby in her arms.

So the last of the Corps of Discovery went over the Lemhi Pass on August 26th. But cold weather was coming, and they hadn't even started on the tough mountain trails ahead.

Clark was having a hard time finding a passable route down the Salmon River. He was also having trouble finding game to feed his party, so he became sure that the Corps could not descend the mountains in that area. Lewis was at the Shoshone village when he got Clark's letter from down river that the Salmon was impassable. He started trading for horses, and by August 30th, after Clark returned to the village, they had purchased 29. Then they all started out together, heading north.

Chapter 5

OVER THE HILLS TO THE SEA
September 1, 1805 to November 18, 1805

NORTH TO TRAVELER'S REST

The tough going started on the 1st of September, for they had to climb 3000 ft. from the Salmon River up to Lost Trail Pass. The road they followed at the start turned in another direction, and they had to make their own road and cut a path through the brush. Some horses fell down the hillsides and became crippled, and damaged important articles, like their last thermometer (no more temperature readings in their journals). When we went up that road alongside the North Fork of the Salmon in 1992, it looked as though the road builders were geniuses to be able to squeeze the road between the river and the mountain. It must have been a bitter pill for the Corps to have to do all that unnecessary climbing to Lost Trail Pass and then go almost 100 miles north, dropping about 3700 ft., just to go back up over the western mountains after that. (Bitterroot Mountains) I haven't read any of their diaries that tell of the great restaurant and swimming pool with water from a hot spring that is at Lost Trail Pass. When we were there it was a cold rainy day, but the warm water felt so good, even with a cold rain on my head. It is a great place to eat and stay overnight, so don't miss that stop. Wouldn't the Corps have loved it!

There is one thought that goes through my head when I read about the terrible ordeals that they had. Why didn't they give up? Quit? I think of the several times the idea of quitting must have been overpowering. When the barge started back down the river at Mandan after that cold winter. When they didn't know which river to go up at the Maria fork. When they started the portage at Great Falls. When they were reaching the end of the Jefferson River. And now heading back uphill and northward when they wanted to go downhill and westward. Just quit. It took unbelievable character to keep proceeding on.

At Lost Trail Pass they were back on the Continental Divide, which jogs at that point. Rivers flowing down both the north and west slopes ended at the Pacific Ocean. In between those two slopes is the Bitterroot Mountain Range, with the Bitterroot River on the northeast side. So they followed its tributaries northwardly until they came to the first village of Flathead Indians, about 12 miles from the pass. The Flatheads were peaceful and helpful to The Corps. They sold to the Corps 13 more horses, and exchanged seven others. That made 42. Now they were in better shape for the mountains ahead. They had nice traveling for the next four days down the valley to Traveler's Rest, (near Lolo) reaching there September 9th.

We enjoyed our trip down the valley, too, for we stopped at Darby and had great buffalo steaks at noon, with all the trimmings. Our camp was at Traveler's Rest that night too, which is now Lolo, Montana. My only trial that day was to drive by a popular buffet in Missoula (near Lolo) and not go in, because neither my stomach nor our budget allows two big meals a day.

A sign on Highway 93 south of Lolo, Montana.

THE LOLO TRAIL

The Corps stayed at Traveler's Rest all day on September 10th, to hunt and fill their stomachs, for the next day they were to start the western trek over the Bitterroot mountains.

The first part of the Lolo Trail rises about 2000 ft. to Lolo Pass, which took the explorers three days. Just before the pass they saw the Lolo Hot Springs, but did not stop long enough to bathe in them. When we drove over the summit in 1992 we found a Visitor Center, where we got a free cup of coffee and an interesting talk with the ranger. We sure thought of the hungry Corps of Discovery when we were approaching the summit, for we passed a dead deer on the side of the road. Apparently a vehicle had hit it soon before, because it was still very warm, but the only damage marks on it were where its horns should have been. I guess the driver of the vehicle that hit it liked the horns and amputated them. But in 1805, even Drewyer, their best hunter, couldn't find a deer to feed his hungry party.

On September 14th, they somehow got on the wrong trail and followed the headwaters of the Lochsa (Kooskooski) River to the place where the Powell Ranger Station is now, where they camped. This was at elev. 3500 ft. and they had just gone over the pass at 5235 elev. They should have stayed on top of the ridge. They were obliged to kill a colt to eat, and had a little portable soup. Two hunters who had been gone overnight brought in Lewis's horse, which had been lost and left behind. The next morning they went four miles down the river, found it impassable, went back up the mountain eight miles to get on the trail again which was at elev. 6400 ft., and camped. That had been another 2900 ft. climb. There was no water up there but plenty of old snow to make portable soup. That day had been hard on the horses, for many fell and one rolled 20 ft. down among rocks, where it took eight or ten men to get it back on its feet. Clark's desk was smashed. That wrong road had been a lot of hard traveling for nothing.

Chapter 6

WINTERING ON THE PACIFIC - FORT CLATSOP
November 18, 1805 to March 23, 1806

BACK AROUND THE BAY

After all of the Corps got back to camp everyone was ready to start out on the homeward journey. But the storms kept them there another 5 days.

The captains held a council, and had everyone vote on where they thought the best place to spend the winter was; to stay on the north shore or to go across to the south shore (in Oregon) to try to find a more suitable spot. The choice of each person was recorded in the Journals. Five thought the lower Columbia Falls would be best, ten liked the mouth of the Sandy River, but they all wanted first to examine the south shore of the Columbia as it enters the ocean. Sacajawea, (whom Clark nicknamed Janey), wanted to go to a place where there were plenty of potatoes.

This election is an indication of how things were in the relationship between the officers and the enlisted men. There is a complete absence of the Captain Bligh attitude in the way decisions were made and orders were given. But discipline hadn't been a problem since Newman's "mutinous expression" a year before in October. The men sensed that the officers were doing their best to provide for their well being, even under difficult conditions.

Better weather gave them a chance to leave on November 25th, so they headed up river 9 miles and tried to cross to the south side, but failed because of the waves. Then they continued upriver to near Pillar Rock, where they had camped November 7th on their way eastward. The next day they continued upriver again to some islands, and found a more protected place to cross. After buying some wappeto roots from some Indians on the south side, they coasted westward in favorable winds and the current to where Svensen is now. The next day they went along the south side of the river, and got around Tongue Point (east end of Astoria). At that place they were pinned down again by high winds that knocked down some trees around them. Clark and the large canoes were obliged to remain there for 10 days. Lewis and five men set out on the 29th to find a suitable place for a winter camp. They went in the Indian canoe which he had purchased in October. It was small and the only one that could be used in bad weather.

While Lewis was gone, (a week) Clark became sick from the constant diet of pounded salmon. Joe Fields shot an elk on December 2nd, the first elk they had taken on the west side of the Rocky Mountains. Elk were larger than deer, were easier to shoot, and could feed several more men than deer. Lewis's long absence became the "Sorce of no little uneasiness on my part of his probable Situation and Safty," wrote Clark. But Lewis and 3 men returned on the 5th, with the news that they had found an area where there was good hunting, and had killed 6 elk and 5 deer. Two men had been left to "secure"(probably dress and dry) the meat from the elk. Two days later the weather abated, and they all left that miserable camp.

The center of Astoria is just west of that camp and the city has commemorated Captain Gray's 1792 discovery, Lewis and Clark's passing, and the founding of Astoria in 1811, by building the Astoria Column. It is on the city's high hill, and has a commanding view of the countryside. You can look to the southwest and see where the Lewis and Clark River flows by Fort Clatsop. You have to climb 162 steps to get to the top, but the view is worth it.

The Astoria Column in Astoria, Oregon.

FORT CLATSOP

They finally arrived at the site of their winter quarters on December 7, 1805 and started building Fort Clatsop. While Lewis stayed to commence building, Clark, the next day, left for the ocean to locate a site for making salt. The plan was to boil sea water to make salt and use it on their return trip eastward. The ocean was only about 7 miles from camp but it took Clark and his 5 men two days to get through the obstacles; like wide streams, swamps and a pond. While pursuing a large gang of elk, they went through shaking bogs and deep mud up to their hips. They finally met some Clatsop Indians who showed them the best way and took them across the streams in their canoe, and to the seashore. Clark had a chance to amaze the Indians. They asked him if he would shoot a brant (a kind of goose).He shot two for them and then they pointed at small ducks which were much harder to hit. He said he "accidently Shot the head of one off." At their village the Indians gathered around Clark's gun in amazement, saying they did not understand this kind of musket. Then they entertained Clark in their homes with games, and "set before me their best roots, fish and Surup."

By the time Clark returned to the camp on December 10th, Lewis's men had brought in elk meat, the camp had been made more comfortable, and land had been cleared for the building of the fort. Most of the men were healthy, but poor Pryor dislocated his shoulder again, Gibson had dysentery, Werner had a strained knee, and Joe Fields had leg boils. Considering the fact that they had had only 3 clear days in a month and they had been wet making canoes for the down river trip to the ocean.

The closest Lena and I got to the Lolo Trail through the mountains was on Route 12, which follows the Lochsa, Middle Fork, and Clearwater Rivers. The actual trail is a few miles north of the road, and can be traveled by vehicles with 4-wheel drive. Route 12 along the three rivers is a pretty drive if you drive slow enough, otherwise it could be terror. We camped two nights on the Clearwater at one of our favorite camps, at Kamiah, Idaho. It's the Lewis and Clark RV Resort. It has lectures and singing every night and conducts auto caravan trips during the day to local places of interest.

The Corps didn't need their 38 horses any more, but they knew they would on the way home. So they just delivered them to the brothers and son of the chief (Twisted Hair) for safe keeping until spring.

When I first read of that arrangement, I wondered how the captains could be so gullible. Of course they branded the horses, and cut off the fore top of each one, and they made a cache for the saddles (not a very good one). The branding iron must have been lost after that because it was found 87 years later 3 1/2 miles above The Dalles, Oregon. (It may still be in the Oregon Historical Society Museum in Portland.) But the Indian chief undoubtedly had formed a pretty close bond with the captains and thought they were good guys, for he kept his word when the Corps actually did return. Twisted Hair must have been a good guy too.

They were at the canoe camp for 11 days, and didn't proceed on down the river until October 7th. If they weren't all so sick it wouldn't have taken so long to build five canoes. Remember that they only took two or three days to build two canoes after the portage around Great Falls. A sentence in Clark's diary for October 5th, 1805 gives an idea of how their diet effected them. "Capt Lewis and my self eate a supper of roots boiled, which filled us so full of wind, that we were scercely able to Breathe all night feel the effects of it." Almost every man had a stomach ache.

But they recovered enough to make 41 miles the first two days on the river. Then a canoe cracked in some rapids which delayed them a day for patching and drying the wet articles.

They camped on the north side of the river where the Snake River joins the Clearwater at present day Lewiston, Idaho and Clarkston, Washington on October 10th. They had covered 58 miles that day, a record.

Lena and I felt at home in the city of Lewiston, maybe because there was a good buffet there. It was as far west as we were planning to go that summer, because our home in Florida was a long way off. While looking at the map, I noticed we were as far away from home as we were from Hawaii, a place we were planning on visiting on our anniversary the next year. Air fare must be only half as much from Lewiston as from home, so we inquired at Betty's Travel to see if that was true. That was on Monday, and we were on a flight from Lewiston to Honolulu long before dawn on Wednesday. The nice part of that arrangement was that we left our van on the airport parking lot for a week free. We landed a week later at 2 am and we sacked out for the rest of the night right there in the van in the parking lot.

There is an excellent campground on the shore of the Snake River in Lewiston, where we stayed all the rest of our visit. When you are there, stay an extra day to visit the Lapwei Museum, a little east of the city, where they will tell you some interesting things about the Nez Perce Indians, which the Journals call the Chopunnish. I had a taste of camas root while I was at that museum; I had always wondered what it tasted like. But I didn't get enough of it to give me "wind" like it did the explorers. The Nez Perce hospitality was an exciting change for the explorers, especially on their return journey the next year.

The Snake and Columbia Rivers, all the way to tidewater east of Portland, Oregon are not the same now as the explorers found them. There are now eight dams that cover up all the rapids and waterfalls that made so much trouble for the Corps. Cruiseboats and barges can now go from the Pacific Ocean to Lewiston and Clarkston. One of those four barge tows carry as much as 538 trucks in one trip, so the use of the river now is tremendous.

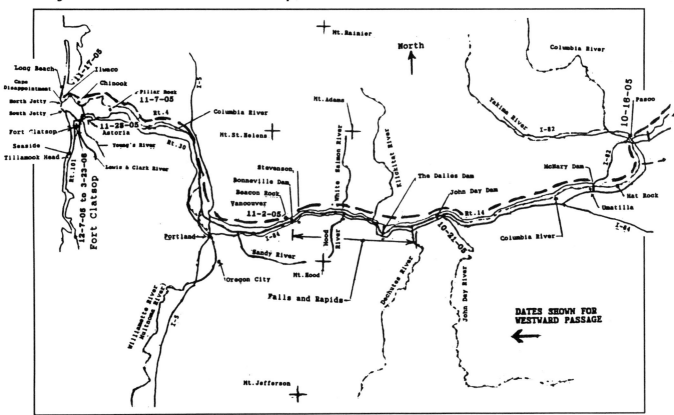

Map 13: Westward Passage, the final leg of the outbound voyage to the sea, late fall 1806.

When the Corps headed downstream from Lewiston on October 11th, the river (the Snake) was larger than the Clearwater had been. The next day they must have passed what is now the Central Ferry State Park in Washington where we once camped. Below that, there were some bad rapids, and one of the canoes overturned and lost some articles.

They reached the Columbia River on October 16th where there were a great number of Indians (probably where the Sacagawea State Park at Pasco, Washington is now), all of them extremely friendly, especially the Great Chief Yellept. The Corps stayed there two nights and had a big ceremony, giving and receiving gifts. They also found out a lot about the Columbia upstream, information that they could send back to Jefferson. Clark and two men paddled 10 miles up to see Indians that showed him where the Yakima River enters the Columbia. He returned to the party late at night. The Corps bought 47 dogs for food while at the forks. At this point they could see Mt. Hood and Mt. Adams, and they recorded their bearings from the confluence.

As they proceeded on down the river, an incident in Clark's diary on October 21st tickled me. Remember that they had used up the last of their spirits two months before. The diary said, "Collins made some excellent beer of the Pasheco quarmash bread of roots which was verry good." The comical thing about that was that Collins made it. He was the man that got 50 lashes at St. Charles and 100 lashes at Kansas City for getting drunk. He must have had a well developed taste for the 'hair of the dog that bites.' He was just showing ingenuity in his own particular way. The bread was getting mouldy and sour so would have had to be thrown away. I like the way that Clark puts double R's in the word 'very'. His realistic spelling really fits in this case.

THE COLUMBIA FALLS

The point where Oregon and Washington are separated by the river was reached on October 19th, and they made good speed until they reached the rapids. They managed to shoot the ones at the John Day's and DeChutes rivers, but about nine miles below that, the falls later known as Celilo Falls, stopped them. After walking ahead, they decided to portage all the supplies about 1200 yards on the north side and portage the canoes 450 yards down the south side. Then they lowered the canoes on ropes the rest of the way down a narrow passage on the south side. They had one canoe get away from them and an Indian got it. He wanted them to pay them for it, which they were obliged to do. A chief reported to them at that time that some of the Indians were planning to kill them so they got their arms ready. No attack.

The captains were interested in the way the Indians processed and preserved fish. They saw, stacked on the rock side of the river, what must have been ten thousand pounds of fish tied up in large bundles. The Indians claimed that the fish are kept sound and sweet for several years.

Lewis saw some well made canoes which the Indians built, so he exchanged a small canoe, a hatchet, and trinkets for one of the Indian canoes. It was a good purchase, for the Corps would use it in some of the high waves that were ahead.

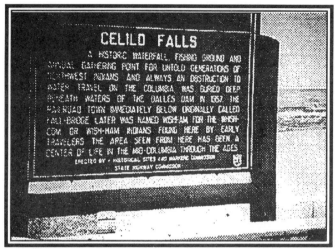

Celilo Falls, were the largest on the Columbia River but are now under the waters of Lake Celilo, above the Dalles Dam.

CELILO FALLS

A historic waterfall, fishing ground and annual gathering point for untold generations of northwest Indians, and always an obstruction to water travel on the Columbia River, was buried deep beneath the waters of the Dalles Dam in 1952. The railroad town immediately below originally called Fall-Bridge later was named Wishram for the Wish-com or Wish-ham Indians found here by early travelers. The area seen here has been a center of life in the mid-Columbia through the ages.

After they had proceeded on only about 2 1/2 miles from the bottom of the above portage, they heard what was a "great roreing." He could see that the wide Columbia had to pass through a channel only 45 yards wide for 1/4 mile, and its velocity was tremendous, with "swelling, boiling and whorling." This was called the Short Narrows. Clark consulted with their best waterman, Peter Cruzat, about their chances at shooting the narrows, and they decided to get those that could not swim to carry the valuables, guns, papers, etc. and they would try to shoot the rapids. This was successful, and they proceeded on until they reached the Long Narrows. These narrows are close to what is now The Dalles, Oregon but are now under water formed by the dams.

They portaged for a mile around the Long Narrows, and then shot the rest, but one canoe filled with water, which detained them three hours before they could proceed on. The canoes were getting pretty beat up so they camped a couple days to get everything patched up and dried. They visited and smoked with the Indians, and danced to Cruzat's fiddling, and had a great time until they headed down river again on October 28th. About two days and 50 miles further they got to the rapids where Cascades and the Bonneville Dam are now.

The rivers of the western slope were heavily populated with Indians, from the time they had met the Nez Perce at the foot of the Bitterroot Mountains, all the way to the sea. The lower Columbia was especially thickly settled, the natives living in substantial houses. These they were proud of, and showed them off to the Corps. Many had guns which they acquired from the ships that put in to the mouth of the Columbia. Some of the women had half-white children; a sure sign that amorous sailors had been there. Most of the Indians were friendly but they were hard traders. They had been accustomed to trading with ships that paid big prices for their wares. The captains saw their trading supplies dwindling after having given to tribes all across the country. These Indians were fussy, wanting blue beads instead of white, and the Corps had none of the blue ones left.

They had to portage around the Grand Shute and other rapids for the next three days, over sloping, slippery banks, sometimes shooting the ones they thought were not too dangerous with empty canoes. These rapids are now under the waters of the Bonneville Dam. Then, at last, they were in tidal water, and all the rapids were past.

Just below the last rapid is a large, 800 ft. high rock on the north side that Clark named Beaten Rock, but has been known since as Beacon Rock. This rock, which has a diameter at the bottom about the same as its height, has been a landmark for river travel since then and now has a beacon to guide airplanes. A foot trail was constructed from 1915 to 1918 up its south side, by Henry Biddle, descendant of the first editor of the Lewis and Clark Journals. (1814 edition). Its easy to see why it took three years to build this trail, for it must have over 60 switchbacks, some of them in groups almost vertical. Climb it some time, and see what the life of a steeplejack is like.

Beacon Rock, in Washington. Tidewater from the Pacific Ocean reaches here. The ocean is 145 miles west of this point.

The view from the top will pay you for the effort. After I came down, I tried to get a picture of the switchbacks, but they are on the south side of the rock, which can only be seen from the river or from the Oregon side with binoculars. The entrance to the trail is easily found; alongside Highway 14 in Washington.

TIDAL WATER, WAVES AND RAIN

Near the present day Portland/Vancouver area, which the Corps reached on November 4th, the Indians told them that in another two days they would meet two ships that were anchored in the bay with white people in them. This did not turn out to be true, but apparently that news spurred them on, for they made 61 miles in the next two days. But it may have actually been true information about the ship, because Capt. Hill in the Lydia, out of Boston, may have been in the river in early November, and left a short time before the Corps arrived.

Then it started to rain, and continued every day for the next 11 days. They could continue only about 65 miles more before the wind and waves in the bay pinned them down on the north shore. On November 7th they were overjoyed because they thought they had seen the ocean ahead, but they were 25 miles from it, which is too far to see because of the curvature of the earth(unless they were standing on a 400 ft. high hill). There were enough waves from the storms to look like the ocean. Their dugout canoes were fine for river waters, but these waves would swamp them quick. So on November 7th they found a place to camp just above the tide, at the bottom of the bluffs, where there was barely enough room to place their mats for sleeping, and this was on round stones. It was just opposite from a 50 foot high, 20 ft. diameter rock a half mile from shore. This is now called Pillar Rock. There is a small lumber yard opposite the Rock now, if you could properly call it a lumber yard. It's at the end of the road east of Altoona. When we saw it, it looked like slim pickings for a campground for the whole Corps.

On the 8th they got into Grays Bay, where Grays River comes in on the north side, and camped at a worse spot than the night before. The tide came up and floated large drifting trees into their camp, endangering the boats. Because the water was salty they had to catch rain water to drink. Their clothes and their tents had begun to get rotten from being constantly wet so they didn't get much protection from the elements. They were fortunate that it was still warm for November.

While Clark was at The November 7th camp, he wrote about the dress of the Wahkiakum Indians. I shouldn't finish this story without copying his writings verbatim. "The Dress of the men differ very little from those above (the upriver Indians), The womin altogether different, their robes are Smaller only Covering their Shoulders & falling down to near the hip- and Sometimes when it is Cold a piec of fur curiously plated and connected So as to meet around the body from the arms to the hips-[Their peticoats are of the bark of the white Cedar] "The garment which occupies the waist and thence as low as the knee before and mid leg behind, cannot properly be called a petticoat, in the common acception of the word; it is a Tissue formed of white Cedar bark bruised or broken into Small Strans, which are interwoven in their center by means of Several cords of the Same materials which Serves as well for a girdle as to hold in place the Strans of bark which forms the tissue, and which Strans, Confined in the middle, hang with their ends pendulous from the waiste, the whole being of Suffcent thickness when the female Stands erect to conceal those parts useally covered from familiar view, but when she stoops or places herself in any other attitudes this battery of Venus is not altogether impervious to the penetrating eye of the amorite. This tissue is Sometimes formed of little Strings of the Silk grass twisted and knoted at their ends" &c. Those Indians are low and ill Shaped all flat heads" That was just part of Clark's entry for November 7, 1805. I'd say he was quite observant.

On the 9th, still pinned down on the north shore, they fought the wind and the waves all day long, trying to protect their canoes from 4 foot diameter, 200 feet long floating trees that almost crushed them. On the 10th they took advantage of a lull in the wind to proceed on about 10 miles, until the wind drove them back 2 miles to the mouth of a small creek. They were tied down here until the 15th. This is near today's Meglar, Washington, but still east of the Astoria Bridge.

THE PACIFIC OCEAN

Lewis decided the only way to get to the ocean was to walk, so he, Drewyer, Joe Fields, and Reuben Fields, and Frazer left to explore the northwest point, called Cape Disappointment, on the morning of the 14th. The next day, Clark saw there was a lull in the storm, so he and the rest of the party set out in the canoes at 3 pm, in a hurry to get around a blustery point, and they found a more comfortable camping spot. This was across the river from where Astoria, Oregon is today. On the 17th, Lewis returned with the news that he had reached the Pacific Ocean. So the Corps of Discovery had fulfilled their goal! This was the end of the west bound voyage.

The next day, Clark, and all the others that wanted to see the ocean, left camp for the Cape, and they also explored the coast a few miles northward.

Cape Disappointment is gorgeous, as it must have been in 1805 when the explorers were there. It's just south of Ilwaco, Wash., and has a Coast Guard Station, two lighthouses, old Fort Canby, and a Lewis and Clark Interpretive Center built on top of the rocks overlooking the Ocean.

The Center has a long winding corridor filled with Lewis and Clark memorabilia, with large windows that let you look down at the Pacific Ocean surf. It is a State run museum but with a budget that can't pay the attendants, so they are volunteers. They are exceptionally enthusiastic and knowledgeable about the Corps of Discovery and seem to enjoy talking about them. I don't know any other Interpretive Center that has such outstanding architecture. One is now being built in Great Falls that might equal it, we will see.

The Coast Guard station is the one that has the famous boats that go out through the surf at the mouth of the Columbia River. You have probably seen the films of their exploits on television. The two lighthouses can be visited by tourists, and the views from them are wonderful.

I wanted to get a close-up picture of the two jetties that were built in World War 2 to protect the harbor. One juts out from the Oregon shore, and one from Washington. Between the end of each is actually the mouth of the Columbia. To get a good picture I hiked through some thick woods on the south end of the peninsula, to get to the edge of the bluff. I was surprised to see, right on the edge, there in the woods, an old fortification, with old gun

I found this fort in the woods on a bluff. Just beyond this fort is where Lewis and Clark first saw the Columbia River enter the Pacific Ocean.

The Columbia River forces its way into the Pacific Ocean here. The Columbia flows from left to right in this photo. The jetties were built during World War II.

emplacements and ammunition caves, all grown up with brush and trees, as if it had been abandoned for years. I carefully walked through it, hoping I wouldn't fall through some ancient shaft or well, to the edge of the embattlements, and got a great picture of the jetties below. Then I got out of there quick, before someone caught me in restricted territory, and slapped uncomfortable bracelets on me. That hill must have been the exact spot that Lewis, and then a few days later Clark, stood when they realized that the main goal of their expedition had been accomplished. The fort hadn't been built then, but it probably was the same place, at the same height above the sea. If Cape Disappointment hadn't already been named, they might have called it Cape Satisfaction.

Chapter 6

WINTERING ON THE PACIFIC - FORT CLATSOP
November 18, 1805 to March 23, 1806

BACK AROUND THE BAY

After all of the Corps got back to camp everyone was ready to start out on the homeward journey. But the storms kept them there another 5 days.

The captains held a council, and had everyone vote on where they thought the best place to spend the winter was; to stay on the north shore or to go across to the south shore (in Oregon) to try to find a more suitable spot. The choice of each person was recorded in the Journals. Five thought the lower Columbia Falls would be best, ten liked the mouth of the Sandy River, but they all wanted first to examine the south shore of the Columbia as it enters the ocean. Sacajawea, (whom Clark nicknamed Janey), wanted to go to a place where there were plenty of potatoes.

This election is an indication of how things were in the relationship between the officers and the enlisted men. There is a complete absence of the Captain Bligh attitude in the way decisions were made and orders were given. But discipline hadn't been a problem since Newman's "mutinous expression" a year before in October. The men sensed that the officers were doing their best to provide for their well being, even under difficult conditions.

Better weather gave them a chance to leave on November 25th, so they headed up river 9 miles and tried to cross to the south side, but failed because of the waves. Then they continued upriver to near Pillar Rock, where they had camped November 7th on their way eastward. The next day they continued upriver again to some islands, and found a more protected place to cross. After buying some wappeto roots from some Indians on the south side, they coasted westward in favorable winds and the current to where Svensen is now. The next day they went along the south side of the river, and got around Tongue Point (east end of Astoria). At that place they were pinned down again by high winds that knocked down some trees around them. Clark and the large canoes were obliged to remain there for 10 days. Lewis and five men set out on the 29th to find a suitable place for a winter camp. They went in the Indian canoe which he had purchased in October. It was small and the only one that could be used in bad weather.

While Lewis was gone, (a week) Clark became sick from the constant diet of pounded salmon. Joe Fields shot an elk on December 2nd, the first elk they had taken on the west side of the Rocky Mountains. Elk were larger than deer, were easier to shoot, and could feed several more men than deer. Lewis's long absence became the "Sorce of no little uneasiness on my part of his probable Situation and Safty," wrote Clark. But Lewis and 3 men returned on the 5th, with the news that they had found an area where there was good hunting, and had killed 6 elk and 5 deer. Two men had been left to "secure"(probably dress and dry) the meat from the elk. Two days later the weather abated, and they all left that miserable camp.

The center of Astoria is just west of that camp and the city has commemorated Captain Gray's 1792 discovery, Lewis and Clark's passing, and the founding of Astoria in 1811, by building the Astoria Column. It is on the city's high hill, and has a commanding view of the countryside. You can look to the southwest and see where the Lewis and Clark River flows by Fort Clatsop. You have to climb 162 steps to get to the top, but the view is worth it.

The Astoria Column in Astoria, Oregon.

FORT CLATSOP

They finally arrived at the site of their winter quarters on December 7, 1805 and started building Fort Clatsop. While Lewis stayed to commence building, Clark, the next day, left for the ocean to locate a site for making salt. The plan was to boil sea water to make salt and use it on their return trip eastward. The ocean was only about 7 miles from camp but it took Clark and his 5 men two days to get through the obstacles; like wide streams, swamps and a pond. While pursuing a large gang of elk, they went through shaking bogs and deep mud up to their hips. They finally met some Clatsop Indians who showed them the best way and took them across the streams in their canoe, and to the seashore. Clark had a chance to amaze the Indians. They asked him if he would shoot a brant (a kind of goose).He shot two for them and then they pointed at small ducks which were much harder to hit. He said he "accidently Shot the head of one off." At their village the Indians gathered around Clark's gun in amazement, saying they did not understand this kind of musket. Then they entertained Clark in their homes with games, and "set before me their best roots, fish and Surup."

By the time Clark returned to the camp on December 10th, Lewis's men had brought in elk meat, the camp had been made more comfortable, and land had been cleared for the building of the fort. Most of the men were healthy, but poor Pryor dislocated his shoulder again, Gibson had dysentery, Werner had a strained knee, and Joe Fields had leg boils. Considering the fact that they had had only 3 clear days in a month and they had been wet

58

most of the time, the sick list could have been a lot longer.

On Friday the 13th, Drewyer and Shannon when hunting, got too eager when they saw a gang of elk, and shot 18 of them. That might have been okay if it had been freezing weather to keep the meat from spoiling. It was too warm for that, so they hurried to finish building a smokehouse, which wasn't operating until the 17th, and it had taken 16 men most of the time to get the elk back to camp. Their diary for December 22nd says that "part of our last Supply of meat is Spoiling from the womph [warmth] of the weather notwithstanding a constant Smoke kept under it day and night." It was entirely spoiled before they moved into the new huts. But they saved and treated the skins, for skins were a valuable commodity for trade with the natives, and for making their own clothes.

All 7 of their huts walls were completed by December 14th, but the roof was a problem, because the wood had to be split into puncheons (boards). They used balsom pine for that which split into 1 1/2 inch thick boards 2 feet wide. Try buying something like that today! They covered the last hut on Christmas Eve, and moved in that night. It must have been a great Christmas, in spite of the rotten elk.

On the 28th, Joe Fields, Bratten, and Gibson were sent to the ocean to set up a salt camp, and commence making

Fort Clatsop, wintering home for the Corps of Discovery, December 7, 1805 to March 23, 1806.

salt. (As I read about this salt camp operation I thought, 'Oh, if they only had had a couple of walky-talky radios'. Think about that as you read the following.) Willard and Wiser went with them to help carry the kettles for the boiling operation, and they were supposed to return to the fort. They hadn't returned on January 3rd, so Gass and Shannon were sent to the salt camp to see about them. When they got to the salt camp on the 6th, they found that Willard and Wiser had left for the fort on the 4th, and their paths had not crossed. Actually Willard and Wiser had got back to the fort on the 5th with a gallon of salt and some whale blubber that the Indians had given to them. Clark was so interested that he, and a party of 14, (including Sacajawea) left the fort on the 6th and arrived at the salt camp on the 7th. To make this story even more complicated, while Lewis was back at the fort wondering why Gass and Shannon had not come back, Clark had put Gass to work making salt, and Shannon was out hunting to provide the salt camp with meat. That left nobody to go back and tell Lewis what was going on.

Clark and party then set out from the salt camp with an Indian guide, to find the whale that had beached itself somewhere south of them. The party of 13 had to struggle for miles over a 1200 ft. high hill that was next to the seashore. (Tillamook Head) This was near present day Cannon Beach. When they got there the whale had already been stripped of all it's blubber by the Tillammok Indians, and all that was left was a 105 ft. long skeleton. Blubber was a very valuable commodity for the Indians, and they were busy boiling it in 20 gallon wooden troughs by placing hot rocks in the blubber. Clark had to use all the merchandise the party had brought with them to procure 300 pounds of blubber and whale oil.

Then they had the problem of getting it all back to the fort, which was 35 miles away and over that steep mountain. The Indians were doing the same thing, for the party met a group of men and women Indians carrying immense loads of blubber and oil. When Clark helped a squaw whose load had slipped, he found that it weighed more than 100 pounds. They arrived at the salt camp that night, January 9th. Clark was "verry much fatigued, more So than I ever was before." I imagine all the men were too.

While writing on January 9, 1806, sitting in the salt camp, Clark reflects on the attitude of the Indian men toward their women and old folks. Of the women, the men "Speak without reserve in their presence, of their every part, and of the most farmiliar Connection. they do not hold the virtue of their womin in high estimation, and will even prostitute their wives and Daughters for a fishing hook or a Stran of beeds" They make them do the drudgery, but then the men also participate. However, they speak freely before the men, and sometimes appear to command with a tone of authority. This is his opinion of the Pacific coast Indians.

When telling, in that days diary, of the Indian treatment of the old men and women, he refers to the Indians along the Missouri River. They treat the old very respectfully, especially those that can still help with the procuring of articles necessary for subsistence. But when they are so infirm that they cannot keep up as the group travels from place to place, they give the poor wretch a little food and water, and tell them they should die and go to their relations who can afford to take care of them. One old man that Clark gave a knife to, claimed to have lived a hundred winters, and he asked for medicine to cure the pain in his back. His grandson told Clark that it was not worth while, for it was time for the old man to die. However, this man was taken care of well with plenty of covering and food; also plenty of attention.

Clark and party left for the fort the next morning at sunrise and reached there at 9 pm, January 10th. This trip must have been relatively easy, because it only took one day. They only had to wade across one 85 yard creek 3 feet deep with a fast, cold current, then cross another creek in a small canoe. Then they met Gibson and Shannon who were carrying 2 elk to the saltmakers, gave them instructions, had trouble with Frazer who lost a knife, portaged

1/4 mile, and hiked down a road through a deep swamp to the canoes that had been hidden. They got into the canoes at sunset, paddled into the bay, then up the Netul River in the dark to the fort. Lewis said "the party returned excessively fortiegued and tired of their jaunt." That figures.

Many Indians visited them at the fort. One was of the Clatsop nation who was apparently half white with red hair; about 25 years old. He had the name 'Jack Ramsey' tattooed on his arm and appeared to understand English, but could not speak it. The men of the Corps collected clothes to give to him.

Most of the Indians stayed overnight at the fort, and became too familiar with the whites. They were losing their respect for the hospitality of the fort. On January 1, 1806 the Orderly Book, signed by both captains, gave orders that all natives must leave the fort at sunset and would not be permitted back in until sunrise. This brought about a change in the attitude of the Indians and they were more respectful thereafter.

While they were at Fort Clatsop they left their canoes on the side of the river, which was not above the highest tide. The men were at times negligent in tying up the canoes, or pulling them up high enough to prevent them drifting out with the receding tide. On January 11th the excellent but smaller canoe was lost, and a larger one that they sometimes called a pirogue went off on January 14th. Luckily 3 men that were sent for it found the pirogue in 3 hours. Lewis said that it would be hard with the few tools they had left, to build three smaller canoes which would carry an equal load to that of the pirogue. It wasn't until February 5th, that Reuben Fields found the good Indian canoe in a marsh when he was out hunting.

Chief Coboway of the Clatsop Indians, whom the explorers called Commowol and Conyear, visited Fort Clatsop frequently and it was to him that the captains left the fort, when they returned eastward in the spring. He made the fort his home for several years after that. 93 years later when historians were looking for the site of the Fort, Coboway's grandson, Silas Smith, assisted in finding its location.

The salt camp did pretty well. They had boiled down seawater to make a bushel by January 25th, according to Collins, who also reported that the salt crew hadn't shot any game, and were living on whale blubber that they bought from the natives. He was sent back to the salt camp with merchandise that they could use to buy provisions from the Indians. Howard and Werner brought this bushel of salt back to the fort 3 days later. Another bushel was brought in on February 3rd, and 2 kegs full were reported on February 17th to be at the salt camp. The captains decided that they had enough to last them as far as the Missouri River, where they could get some more, so they ordered the salt camp evacuated. Ordway and party had the salt and kettles back to the fort on February 21st. Total salt was 20 gallons.

Probably having a sufficiency of salt wasn't the only reason for stopping the saltmaking. Willard had shot 4 elk on February 8th, and cut his knee with a tomahawk, so couldn't bring all the meat to the salt camp; nor could he continue his duties making salt. He went back to the fort and told that Bratton was unwell, and Gibson was so sick he couldn't walk. Pryor and 4 men went to carry Gibson back from the salt camp. They returned with Gibson on a litter on February 15th. Bratton walked back, but was sick. These two remained sick for as long as they were at Fort Clatsop. Besides those two, 4 others were reported on the sick list on February 22nd.

The old pile of rocks that were there at the salt camp when the explorers went back to the fort stayed there until 1900 when the Oregon Historical Society reestablished the site, and the furnace was rebuilt. The exact location was proved by Jenny Michel, a Clatsop Indian, [1816-1905] who remembered her mother's story of white men that boiled water there. It is in the south end of Seaside, Oregon just a few house lots from the beach. The story of the salt project is told on an engraved bronze plaque near the furnace.

Replica of the Lewis and Clark saltmaking furnace on the Pacific shore, a day's hike from Fort Clatsop.

Clark spent a lot of time during the winter making maps of the territory they had explored in almost 2 years since they left the Mississippi River. Because they had not, of course, explored up all the rivers, they had questioned the natives about what territory each river drained and in what direction it flowed. The only river that they had missed was the Williamette River, because its waters entered the Columbia behind an island in the river on the south side. On their descent the Corps went down the north side of that island. Their conversations with the Indians made them resolve to chart this river, which they called the Multnomah, on their way upriver.

The Indians had good memories. They told the captains the number of masts on about 13 ships that put in to the mouth of the river, and the masters name of each. These names lost something from their pronunciation, but they did sound a bit like real masters that had sailed into the Columbia. They told when the ships had been there, and when to expect them again, although historians cannot corroborate all their stories. They told of one trader that killed a great many elk, and another that fired on them from the ship and killed several Indians.

On March 6th, Pryor and 2 others left in a canoe to go up the Columbia to where the Indian fishermen lived to try to buy some fish, because the hunters were having trouble finding elk. On March 11th he returned with a boatload of fish, but he was in a borrowed Indian canoe. What had happened to his canoe? While he was at the village he tied it up with a hide cord, which the Indian dogs then chewed up, and the pirogue drifted off. They borrowed the one they were in, and on the way back they found the lost canoe. They had to leave it until they had returned the Indians canoe. This load of fish, brought in on March 11, gave the Corps a big lift. Lewis said, "we once more live in clover; Anchovies fresh Sturgeon and Wappetoe." The captains thought the reason for the many sick men had been because of the poor diet. This fish probably did get them in better physical condition for the March 23rd departure.

The captains were always fair in their dealings with the natives, but there is a canoe acquisition that takes some thinking before deciding if it was fair or not. On February 3rd Drewyer and LaPage killed 7 elk up on Point Adams, so Pryor and 5 men went after them the next day. When they reached the elk, 5 had been stolen by the Clatsops, so they could only bring 2 back to camp. The captains didn't forget this incident. On the 12th, a Clatsop man who must have had a guilty conscience, brought 3 dogs to the fort to pay for the stolen elk, but the dogs promptly ran away. When a canoe lost on a hunting trip by Sheilds, Reuben Fields, and Frazer couldn't be found, the captains knew they would have to buy another canoe before they could leave for home. The Clatsops wouldn't sell them a canoe for a reasonable price because they knew the captains wanted one badly. We have unscrupulous businessmen like that today. They make you mad when you are at their mercy and they keep raising their prices. So the captains decided (as proposed by one of the interpreters), to steal one of their canoes because of the elk that had been stolen from them. So 4 men went out and got one from the river at Point Adams prairie and concealed it near the fort until the day of their departure. They almost got away with it, but not quite. Later, after their departure from Fort Clatsop, on the second day of their trip upriver, a Cathlahmah Indian said that the stolen canoe was his, but he consented to take an elk skin for it, and they proceeded on.

A party of Chinook Indians arrived March 15th, set up a camp near the fort and laid siege to the men of the Corps of Discovery. The trouble with that was that it was a chief, his wife and 6 women, who were out to market the men. They were the same women that had visited the Corps in November, when they were on the north side of the Columbia, and had given several of the men venereal disease. Lewis had been trying all winter to cure the men with mercury, (of all things) and thought that most of them were cured. The captains faced this threat by getting all the men to promise to leave the women alone this time. After 3 days the captains said that they believe "notwithstanding every effort of their winning graces, the men have preserved their constancy to the vow of celibacy." So the chief and women departed, with no gain but a certificate of deportment for the chief, presented by the captains with a list of the names of the men of the Corps and a brief history of their trip via the Missouri and Columbia Rivers, that they could show to the next ship that put in to the river. Similar certificates were given to the chiefs of the other tribes. The Indians actually did show one of those certificates to the captain of the next ship that visited them, which was less than three months later. The ship did not get back to the United States with the news until after Lewis and Clark reached St. Louis.

When you visit the reconstructed Fort Clatsop, and walk down to the riverfront where they stored their canoes, and see where the spring was that they got their water from, you will get an intimate feeling for their life there. The interesting staff at this Interpretive Center will assist you in this experience.

The Corps of Discovery loaded their canoes and departed Fort Clatsop at 1 o'clock on March 23, 1806, having sent Drewyer and the Fields brothers on ahead the day before, to hunt and to meet the party near where Astoria is today. The captains wrote that they had lived as well since December 7th as they had any right to expect, in spite of the rain that had fallen almost constantly since their arrival.

Chapter 7

UP THE COLUMBIA
March 23, 1806 to April 30, 1806

The first day the Corps left Fort Clatsop they rounded Point Williams, and then Tongue Point, with today's Astoria in between, and camped on the John Day River. There are two rivers with the name John Day. The other one is east of Biggs, Oregon. At this one, east of Astoria, they met up with Drewyer and the Fields brothers, who had been sent ahead to hunt. They had shot 2 elk, so 15 of the party went out the next morning to bring them in.

Bratten, who had been down with back trouble, was unable to assist in his regular work duties, so he had to be constantly helped. This continued all the way to the mountains for the poor guy before he was healed. The other two saltmakers fared a little better. Gibson was sick, too but his recovery was sooner than Bratten's. Willard, who had cut his knee, had pretty much recovered.

They covered 85 river miles in the first 5 days of paddling upriver. During that time they did a lot of trading with the Indians for food, mostly the Cathlamet tribe. The men enjoyed wappato roots, which is a lot like potato, and the Indians gathered them in huge quantities. Wappato did not disagree with the men like camas roots did, which made them so sick when they first reached the western slopes of the Rockies the autumn before.

Other foods they got from the Indians were anchovies and sturgeon. Today the local fishermen catch a lot of sturgeon in the lower part of the Columbia River, and they are big. When Lena and I camped at Chinook, Wash. a fellow camper was cleaning two giant sturgeons he had just caught. The two covered a picnic table. I'll bet the whole 33 member Corps couldn't eat 2 sturgeon that size at a single setting. It may have been the wrong season for salmon however, when we were there in June, for we didn't see anyone catching them.

As they paddled along they had a lot of company. All the natives had superior canoes to the Corps, and they had a ball following along, and even trading as they proceeded. Most were friendly, but there were many thieves among them, who managed to get away with some of the merchandise that the Corps had remaining for future trading. It got so bad that the captains had to threaten to shoot, to protect their stuff.

They got to Deer Island on March 28, where they repaired their canoes and packed in the venison. The hunters killed 7 deer but the eagles ate up 3 of them in a short time. They shot some of the eagles. They saw a vulture drag a buck deer 30 feet. Maybe the vulture was a condor. Ordway wrote about the snakes on the island, saying, "the Snakes are as thick as the Spears of Grass on this Island." Ordway's other writings haven't shown such exaggeration before.

By the time they reached Sandy River, past present day Portland, they stopped to do some hunting, make some elkskin rope to be used in the swift currents they knew were ahead, and to explore up the Sandy a short distance. They then heard from the Indians that they had passed the Multnoma River, now known as the Williamette River. The reason was because it was on the south side of a long island they had just passed on its north side. They did the same thing going down river in the fall. They knew they couldn't go back to President Jefferson without finding out about this river, so they decided to go back to see it. It was a good thing they did, because the Williamette valley would be a destination for many thousands of people crossing on the Oregon Trail for the next 60 years, and their report triggered a desire in peoples minds all over the country.

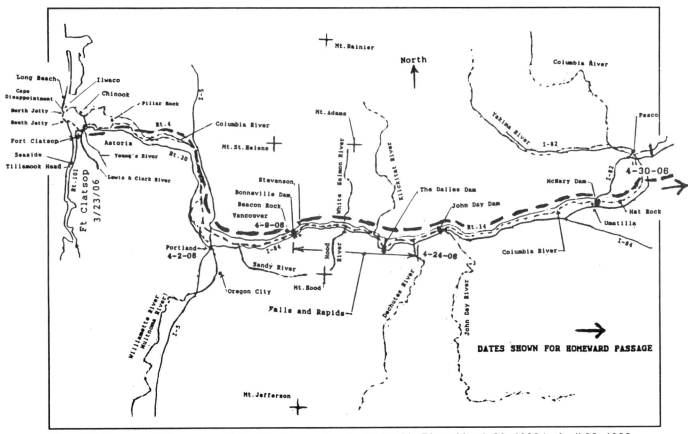

Map 14: Homeward Passage from the Pacific coast up the Columbia River; March 23, 1806 to April 30, 1806.

On April 2nd, Clark took 7 men and an Indian guide back down 20 miles along the south side of the river to the confluence of the Williamette. On the way they passed the Indian guide's village, and then stopped at another village near where Clark saw about a hundred small canoes laying in the woods. They were about 14 ft. long and 18 to 24 inches wide, (like kayaks) and were owned by Indian women that lived near the rapids upriver. They used them occasionally to gather wappeto. These roots grow in shallow water and the squaws harvest them with their feet, bring them to the surface, and throw them into the canoes.

Clark tried to buy some wappeto at the village, but was rejected, and the Indians were sulky. Then he did some magic tricks. He threw what he called port fire match, into the fire, which changed the color of the fire, and when the Indians cried for him to put it out, he just let it go out by itself. He also showed them his compass which was magic to them, and they put wappeto at his feet. He paid them well for it, and then smoked with them before leaving. Then he and his crew explored the lower part of the Williamette, measured the depth and width, and he was back up the river to Lewis camp the next evening. His route probably took him right through what is now downtown Portland. I hope he had an easier time than Lena and I did when we tried to drive through downtown Portland. It is now a veritable maze, because of the one way streets. We went round and round for awhile until suddenly we were out one end.

The first 5 days of April in 1806 they had zero river miles in their log, for they camped where there was a lot of game. There were also 3 cub bears which Collins and Windsor captured alive and brought back to camp. These were sold to the Indians for pets in exchange for more wappeto roots. There wasn't enough sun to dry the meat so they had to do it over their fires. They were preparing for the hard upriver travel and desert ahead. At that camp they were within 35 miles of the first rapids.

On the 9th of April they passed, on the south side, beautiful Multnoma Falls, the prettiest falls we've seen anyplace, unless maybe Yosemite Falls in California. Neither of those have an amount of water to compare with Niagara Falls or the Yellowstone Falls, but the graceful way the water comes down is what makes them spectacular. I wrote in my diary, "An awesome sight." Interstate 84 goes right by it and has a convenient exit.

They got to the first rapids which they had called the Grand Shute, just upriver from Beacon Rock, where the Bonneville Dam is today, and prepared to tackle them on the 9th. They were busy portaging over the first group of badwater until the 13th, when they got back in their canoes, and proceeded on. They were constantly heckled by thieves from the Wahclellah tribe, while they were trying to portage. On the 11th, when two of the men were attempting to pull up one of the canoes and were a little detached from the others, one of the natives from the audience of Indians watching from the hills, threw stones down at them. Thompson detected an Indian in the act of stealing an axe, and had to wrestle with him to get it away from him. Lewis's dog, Seaman, was stolen, and three men were able to chase and threaten the thieves, until they let it go. Another time, Sheilds found himself at a distance from his companions, and had to draw his knife against one of the Indians, before the man could discharge his arrow. Colter retrieved a tomahawk that had been stolen from Clark on last November 4th, just below Beacon Rock, when they were on their way down river. The captains didn't want to use violence against these people, but Lewis said, "our men seem well disposed to kill a few of them."

They had lost two canoes during the portage by crashing against the rocks, so Lewis went ahead to the village of the Yehhuh Indians (across from Carson, Wash), to buy two new ones for 4 elk skins and 2 robes. Meanwhile, Clark took the two heavily laden pirogues up the north shore to look for the hunters that had been sent ahead to the Cruzat River, (now Wind River) two days before, but couldn't find them. So he continued six more miles upriver, where Lewis joined him with the two new canoes. Then they proceeded on another 12 miles.

They must have been getting fed up with the battles against the current, even after only 5 days of heavy work. They knew there would be months of this slow going ahead, if they had to go all the way by water. They found themselves in the same situation as they were in the fall before, when they were on the way up the Jefferson River. The question in their minds was, "How can we get horses?"

At a village near present day White Salmon, on April 14th, they saw the first horses they had seen since last fall, but no one would sell them any until they reached the village near the Dalles area. Clark dickered for 2 days, and then bought the first three on April 17th. Charbonneau also bought a nice mare. Because they knew that the Celilo Falls were ahead, the captains figured that if they could get the baggage on horses as soon as possible they wouldn't have to portage their canoes around the falls. Besides that, they would have to have as many horses as possible eventually, to get over the mountains. So buying horses was the main project. The men were also busy making pack saddles for any horses they might be able to buy.

Before the long narrows there was a 200 ft. length of fast water where they were able to pull the empty canoes up with a cord, and then carry the baggage up. When they got to the long narrows, the water was so high they had to cut the larger pirogues up for fuel because it was impossible to pull them up. The Indians would give nothing for them.

Clark was staying with the Skillute Indians while he was trying to trade unsuccessfully for more horses. The chief had a wife who was termed "a sulky Bitch," but had pains in her back. Clark wrote that he, "rubed a little camphere on her temples and back, and applyed worm flannel to her back which she thought had nearly restored her to her former feelings. this I thought a favourable time to trade with the chief who had more horses than all the nation besides." The chief sold him two more horses.

The arrival of the salmon on April 19th put the natives in a good mood, and five more horses were purchased. That would have made them have a total of eleven, but Willard let one run away, and some other deals didn't work out. One horse was needed to carry Bratten, because he still had back trouble and couldn't walk. The other horses were used to help in the portage around the Long Narrows, and it was soon completed. Clark and 4 others went upriver to the Enesher village to buy more horses, but after two days he couldn't buy a single one. Thievery was all he got from those rascals. The Corps didn't need 3 of the canoes any more so they traded 2 of them to the Eneshers for beads, and they cut up the 3rd one for firewood, which was scarce in that area.

They proceeded on, both horses and canoes, to Celilo Falls on April 21st, and quickly carried the remaining 2 small canoes to the upper level. Then they all went up about 4 miles to a point opposite the DeChutes River, where they camped 1/2 mile from another Enesher village. Earlier that morning, Lewis had lost his temper when he caught an Indian stealing an iron canoe fitting, and struck him several severe blows; then he reminded the chiefs that he had the power to kill them all and burn their houses, but it "was not my wish to treat them with severity provided they would let my property alone. that I would take their horses if I could find out who had stolen the tommahawks, but that I had reather loose the property altogether than take the ho(r)se of an inosent person." The chiefs hung their heads and said nothing.

On the 22nd, in spite of having a horse run away and having a confrontation with more thieves, they got 14 miles further upriver, getting used to overland traveling. And they bought another horse.

A deal was made on the 24th with a Chopunnish (Nez Perce) Indian who was traveling with his family in the same direction, to hire three of his extra horses. Three more were purchased from the Wahhowpums. Now they were ready to sell their last two canoes to some Indians who had said they would give them a horse for them. When these prospective buyers found out that the Corps were planning on going only by land, they thought they would get the canoes for nothing. When they saw Drewyer start to chop them up, they quickly offered some beads for them, which was accepted, and the chopping stopped. That is what I call brinkmanship trading.

Lena and I camped for a few days at the Marina at Umatilla, across the river from the place that the Corps reached on April 26, 1806. By that time they had a horse to carry each of the men's packs, and two more for the captains to ride. Also one for Bratten.

They had made 48 miles in the last two days. I thought of them when we saw the pleasure cruise ship that docked at Umatilla when we were there. Wouldn't they have been amazed? This was just below the McNary Lock and Dam, and next to the Interstate 82 bridge. The ship then went up through the locks on its way up the Snake River to Lewiston and Clarkston, two cities named for the captains. This is where the Corps was headed.

A long march on the next day, got them to Chief Yellept's Wallawalla Indian tribe. It was across the river from the confluence of the Walla Walla River, which is 16 miles below the entrance of the Snake River. Yellept had helped the Corps so much when they were there in the fall. Now he gave Clark an elegant white horse, really wanting cooking pots in return, but what pots they had were needed, so Clark gave him his sword and a hundred balls and powder. Yellept told of a good road that led from a point across the river to the south side of the Kooskooske River (Clearwater River, near Clarkston), which they decided they would take. They asked Yellept to lend them canoes to cross the river and he agreed, but only if they would stay another day to visit, which they were obliged to do. They swam their horses over that night, hobbled them, and left them there overnight. A neighboring tribe, the Yakimas, were invited to a party, 100 came, and a great social evening was had by all. The Corps danced to Cruzat's fiddle and the Indians danced for the men. Some of the Corps even joined in the Indian dance. These were well behaved people, and the party was over at 10 pm, when everyone went home happy.

While they were with the Wallawallas, Clark was asked to heal many of the natives. One had a broken arm which he tied up with sticks for splints. Others had fevers, pains, and sore eyes. One brought his wife who had a violent cold and a fever. He also brought a horse as a present. Clark said he gave her "medesene as would keep her body open and raped her in flannel." They also left eye medicine with the tribe because eye trouble was very prevalent with all the natives in that region. They wrote that this was, "1 G(rain) of Ela v V.& 2 g. of Sacch S to an ounce of water and in that proportion." What that supposedly is, is calaminae vitriolum, which you couldn't prove by me, but I certainly wonder how they ever got a chemical like that 200 years ago. Besides that, how did they have it in sufficient quantities to give so freely of it to so many Indians? They had carried the stuff 5000 miles, were often out of food, and yet they had eye water to spread around. Amazing!

According to a footnote I read in Ordway's journal, written by Milo Quaife, there was a fifteen year old Indian girl at that village that lived to the age of 111 years. She remembered the "medical ministrations" of the white captains, because her father's lame leg was treated by them.

The next morning, the Indians loaned them canoes to take themselves and baggage over to the east side of the Columbia, upriver from where the Walla Walla River enters the Columbia, where they camped. This place is now Madame Dorion Memorial Park, named for an Iowa Indian woman, who came west with her husband and two children, less than six years after the Corps was there. They came to establish a trading post, but when the men with them started trapping, the Bannock Indians killed them. She and her two kids hid in the Blue mountains, and got to safety in the spring.

Chapter 8

TO NEZ PERCE AND LOLO TRAIL
April 30, 1806 to June 30, 1806

That was the last that Lewis and Clark saw of the Columbia River, for they started eastward up the Touchet River on April 30th. Three days travel got them to Dayton, Wash, on May 2nd, which was about the upper end of the Touchet River. Route 124 and 12 now follow this trail from about Prescott, to beyond Dayton, and we could see the river as we drove along. We left the trail there for overnight, because we wanted to camp on the Snake River at Central Ferry State Park. But as we left Route 12 onto Route 127 at Dodge, a grass

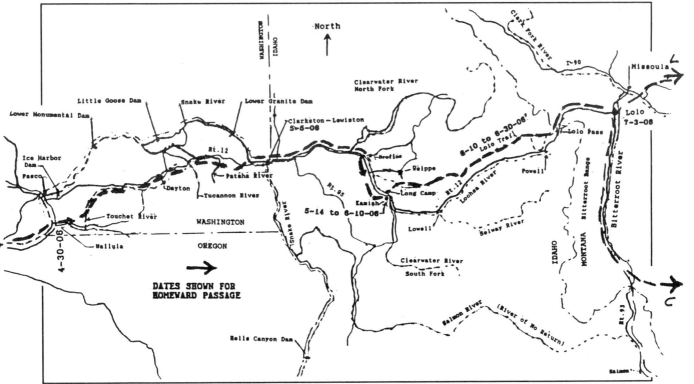

Map 15: Homeward Passage, eastern Washington and western Idaho, along the Lolo Trail in late spring and early summer of 1806.

fire at the junction racing up the hill toward us made me floor the accelerator to get out of there quick. Firemen were there working on it. When we returned to that area the next morning all the hills there were black, but the fire was out. But the campground at Central Ferry hadn't been endangered and it was beautiful.

The next day the Corps struck out over a high plain to the Tucannon River, where they dined. Then over another high plain down to the Pataha Creek, which they followed a few miles upstream and camped. They made 28 miles that day, even though the weather was miserable. It rained, hailed, snowed and blew with "Great Violence" most of the day. The wind was at their back, so maybe it pushed them.

They were pleased on May 3rd, to meet Chief Wearkkoompt (Big Horn) and ten of his Nez Perce nation who had been so friendly with them in the fall. He had come a considerable distance to meet them. The next day they all went 8 miles down hill to the Snake River, at a point 7 1/2 miles below Lewiston/Clarkston and the Clearwater/Snake confluence.

The Nez Perce living on the river advised them that the road on the north side, up the Clearwater River, was much better. So, on the evening of May 4th, they swam the horses across, and with Indian canoes, carried their baggage across. Chief Big Horn left them then, because his village was on the south side.

From the Snake-Clearwater confluence to the entrance of the North Fork of the Clearwater (Colters Creek), there were a lot of Indian villages that remembered Clark as a doctor, because he had treated their illnesses last fall. The natives refused to sell the Corps any food, but when he started treating them again, they became more generous, and the Corps was able to obtain horses, dogs and roots for food.

Clark felt guilty (knowing he wasn't a real doctor, I suppose) because he thought that he was deceiving the natives, but the natives claimed they were healed. He removed abscesses, dressed wounds, set splints, and applied liniments. He used flour of sulphur, cream of tarter, basilicon, balsam capiva, medicine for rheumatism, and of course lots of eye water. Lewis was very proud of Clark's good name among the Indians; he writes, "My friend Capt. C. is their favorite phisician and has already received many applications." Both captains agree to take care to give them no article that can possibly injure them.

In spite of how friendly the Chopunnish (Nez Perce) were, one of them made Lewis again lose his temper. This Indian thought it was terrible for the Corps to eat dogs, so when he saw Lewis eating dog meat on May 5th, he took a live puppy and threw it into Lewis's plate and laughed. Lewis threw it back at him, struck him, and threatened him with his tomahawk. Then he went back to eating dog.

Another dark happening came on the next day. The journals report that there was a quarrel between Drewyer and Colter over the duty of leading a horse. There were probably many small quarrels between the men in 2 1/2 years of being closely together, but none were serious enough to get into the journals like this (except maybe the time that Charbonneau struck his wife Sacagawea). I wondered if they ever were friends again, for they were only together after that until July 3rd, and then another 9 days before Colter was discharged. They must have got over this, for they later on were together, with Manuel Lisa, when he formed a fort on the Yellowstone River.

On the 7th, they crossed the Clearwater to the south side again, because the guide said the trail was better, and there was more game on that side. Then they went upriver to what they called Mosquito Creek, and camped at an old Indian camp.

The question that was undoubtedly on the captains mind since last fall when they left their 38 horses with Twisted Hair was, "Where are they now, we need them?" Chief Cut Nose was traveling with them as they met Twisted Hair. Instead of greeting them, he was very cool, and then spoke in a loud voice, angrily. Cut Nose answered him the same way, and the two started an argument. The captains found out later that it was about the Corps' horses; also about saddles, which the Corps had deposited in a cache side of the river, but had been uncovered by a change in the flow of the river. Cut Nose did not like the way Twisted Hair had used the horses for his own good during the winter, and that they had become scattered. The captains left them to argue and proceeded on another few miles and camped. The two chiefs formed separate camps, both in ill humor. The captains sent Drewyer to Twisted Hair's camp to ask him to come and talk about the horses, which he did.

Twisted Hair agreed that the horses were scattered, but that he would help find them and deliver as many it was possible to get. He also told the captains that he had rescued some of the saddles and they were now in another cache. The captains expressed their regrets that there should be a misunderstanding between the chiefs. The Cut Nose said, in Twisted Hair's presence, that he was a bad old man, and that Chief Broken Arm, the high chief, had forbid Twisted Hair from taking care of the horses. In spite of this sort of talk, the following night the two chiefs camped together, apparently friends again.

The Corps went 6 miles and camped at Twisted Hair's Lodge one day and then headed the next day, May 10th, for Broken Arm's lodge, about 16 miles away. It had been snowing and there was 8 inches of snow on the high plains, and it was very slippery. For this trip they had 21 more horses, because Twisted Hair had already delivered that many to the captains. When they descended 800 ft. to the Lawyer Creek bottom where Broken Arm's lodge was, there was no snow, and an American Flag was flying in front of the lodge. It was the flag that had been left the previous fall with Twisted Hair, to be given to the high chief who was away at war at the time.

Chief Broken Arm met them under the flag, with a warm welcome, and presented them with a bushel of camas, 4 cakes of bread, dried fish, and, to the captains surprise, two fat horses to eat. This sure made the very hungry Corps happy. A large lodge (tent) was pitched and Lewis and Clark were invited into it to be used as their home while visiting the chief. A fire was built in the center and fresh wood was left at the door. These Indians (Nez Perce) knew how to be really hospitable. The funny part of this lodge for the captains, was that when they got up in the morning the floor was covered with sleeping Indians all around them.

The next day they had a council that took most of the day. The lodge was filled with chiefs, for another one showed up with a name that meant five big hearts. The interpreting was complicated. The words had to go through French and Minnetare (Charbonneau and Drewyer), Shoshone, (Sacagawea to another Shoshone boy) and then into Nez Perce. The replies had to reverse the procedure. The captains gave medals and gifts and showed off their magnets, spy glass, compass, watch, and air gun. Then the Corps went to work healing the sick.

One of their sick was a pathetic case; 4 Indians on May 11th, carried on a robe, a paralyzed chief to Clark, and set him down before him. The man remained in the position he was left in, unable to move, and had been that way for 5 years. He was to be a continuous patient of Clark's until June 8th, and his progress was reported in the journals almost every day until then.

When Clark had finished administering to the sick, about noon on the 13th, they collected their horses and headed down Lawyer Creek to the Clearwater, and waited for canoes of Chief Broken Arm which were to carry them over the river. They were to make a more permanent camp on the east side, at a location suggested by Broken Arm. Heavy snow in the mountains would hold them there until it melted sufficiently for them to proceed on towards home. The canoes did not arrive until late that night, so they camped near where

Today there is a lumber company on the east side of the river where the Long Camp was.

Kamiah, Idaho is now, on the west side of the river. The next morning, after getting their baggage over, they swam the horses, and went about a mile downstream on the east side, to where an ancient Indian fortification had been. They wouldn't leave this place for almost a month. This would be a waiting time, and their main task was to keep themselves healthy, and prepare every day for the impending problem of getting over those rough mountains. They watched the weather carefully, always hoping for warm temperatures to melt those mountain snows.

Lewis's attitude was interesting. He wrote on May 17th, "I am pleased at finding the river rise so rapidly, it now doubt is attributeable to the mel(t)ing snows of the mountains; that icy barrier which separates me from my friends and Country, from all which makes life esteemable.- patience, patience."

Their horses were giving them trouble while they were setting up camp. The stallions were wild and were causing such commotion that the men decided to castrate them. An Indian volunteered to do the job, for the Indian's system was better than the way Drewyer had operated on some of the other horses. One of the horses had became infected from the operation and had to be shot. Several of the troublesome ones, in spite of castration, had to be shot and eaten. All the horses were driven closely together the next day so they would become familiar with each other. This is always necessary when new animals are put together.

We saw that same procedure one day in Montana. We watched cowboys round up over a thousand cattle that had been brought together from different pastures. The cowboys on their horses, almost a dozen of them, remained almost motionless around the herd while their trained dogs chased any errant cows back into the pack. They were held together for several hours until they got comfortable with each other. Lewis and Clark's horses were more wild, so they had to be brought together the same way each day for several days, before they would stay together as a group.

At the Corps new camp, now called Long Camp, huts were built with sticks and grass roofs, that kept out the rain well. Collins shot 2 bear the first day on that side of the river, LaBiche shot a bear and 2 cubs, and he and Shannon came back with 2 pheasants apiece. So the food situation began to look good. Bear meat was a rarity for the Indians, who did their hunting with bows and arrows, so the fifteen Indians that were visiting at the camp considered it a treat when they were given 2 shoulders and a ham from the bear, for them to eat. This was the Corps way of paying for past favors and gifts.

Everyone was kept busy. Hunters were always sent out in pairs, as protection from the dangerous bears, and each pair was sent in opposite directions. Five men were engaged in making a canoe that could be sold when they left, and also used in passing the river; for the Indians on the west side sold roots that were a part of the Corps diet now. Camas roots still made some of them sick, but Sacagawea kept bringing in roots from a fennel plant that kept the wind-making properties of camas in check. Building the canoe was a good idea, but after finishing it on the 26th, they lost it on the 30th, when fast current overturned and sank it with valuable merchandise aboard.

The baby Pomp became sick on May 22nd, with a high fever, and swelling of the back of his neck and jaw, and he would get better and then worse for most of the time they were at the Long Camp. The captains administered every cure that they knew of, and tried to make him comfortable. He was cutting teeth during this sickness, which probably gave him additional misery. By June 8th he had nearly recovered.

The most interesting activities at the Long Camp was the remarkable healing of both Bratten and the paralyzed Indian chief. Bratten was still in violent pain at times, and he could hardly get around. He couldn't even sit up straight. On May 23rd, John Sheilds observed that he had seen men in a similar situation restored by violent sweats. Bratten requested it be tried on him. Sheilds dug a 3 ft diameter, 4 ft deep hole, and built a large fire in it to heat the ground to a high temperature. Then he put a board at the bottom, and another above that for a seat. An arched roof was built to go over it. They lowered Bratten into this hole, and gave him a vessel of water to sprinkle on the hot walls. The steam from this made the heat almost unbearable for him. After 20 minutes of this, he was taken out and plunged into cold water twice, before putting him back in the hole for 45 minutes. While there, he was given a great deal of horse mint tea, whatever that was. Then he was wrapped in blankets, so he would cool gradually. The next day he said the pain had almost gone. By June 5th, he was sent with Colter on a trading mission to the Indians. The men liked Bratten. Remember, he came in second in the voting for a sergeant to take Floyd's place, when Sgt. Floyd died in 1804.

Good news got around quick, for at eleven o'clock on the 24th, a canoe came from across the river with three natives and the chief that had lost the power of his limbs. The sweat hole was prepared for him, but he couldn't be put in the hole, because he couldn't hold himself or sprinkle the water on the wall. Two days later on May 27th, the old father of the paralyzed chief wanted to get in the hole with his son and hold him while he sweat. This was tried, and when they got out, the son was in pain, for the first time in years. They gave him laudanum, which composed him. The next day he could use his hands and arms, and the following day he could wash his own face, and was excited about his eventual recovery.

The captains planned for him to stay with them so that they could repeat his treatments. After a severe sweat on May 30th he was able to move one leg a little, and move all his toes, and his hands were back to normal. Another treatment on June 5th made him "very languid" but improving, and on June 8th he was able to bear his weight on his legs, and a lot of his strength had returned. That is the last that the journals tell about the man. Sheilds should have been given a degree as an experimental physician.

It is claimed that the World's first Olympic competitions occurred here at Long Camp, between the United States and the Nation of the Chopunnish (Nez Perce). The Nez Perce and the Corps of Discovery did have foot races a couple days before they left the camp. Drewyer and Reuben Fields were the Corps' fastest runners, and there was one Indian that could keep up with them. After the races they were divided into two groups and a strenuous game called prison base was played. The captains were getting the men that hadn't been out hunting and had been getting flabby, in shape for the tough mountain climbing ahead.

All sorts of schemes were used in trading with the Indians, because the Corps supplies were dwindling. McNeal and York were sent across the river on June 2nd with buttons that both Lewis and Clark had cut off their coats, some eye water, and some small empty tin boxes, to see what they could get for them. They returned in the evening with 3 bushels of roots, and some bread, which went over big in camp. Another scheme was the awls that the men made, from links of chains that they took from old beaver traps, and the natives were glad to buy them.

On May 21st, some of the Corps merchandise was distributed to each member, in order for them to buy from the natives their own supplies that they would need on their passage over the mountains. This was mainly for roots, because the men could catch their own fish and shoot their own meat. But roots were more difficult to dig, because the favorite plant, the cows, or cous, looked very much like species of hemlock that were poisonous. The native women were very good at identifying the correct plant.

Chief Hohastillpilp had been good to the Corps. He owned most of the horses that were on the east side of the Clearwater River, and he told the captains that they could have any of them they wanted for food, if they got hungry. No other chief on the whole trip had been so generous. He also heard of where the tomahawk of Sergeant Floyd was, that had been stolen from them last fall as they passed through. The captains wanted it so they could present it to the family of Floyd when they returned. The thief had sold it to a chief, who was now dying, and his wife insisted on burying the tomahawk with the body. This was a long way off to the north but Hohastillpilp and Chief Cut Nose accompanied Drewyer to the place and dickered with the wife. Besides what Drewyer offered, Hohastillpilp threw in two of his horses that the wife could bury with the dead chief. They got the tomahawk, and another one that had been left at one of last falls camps, by one of the captains. Which captain? Lewis's diary says Clark; Clark's diary says Lewis. That gave me a chuckle.

Ordway, Frazer, and Wizer left on May 27th, on horseback, to get some salmon that were supposed to have arrived in the Salmon and Snake Rivers, expecting to return on the next day. But the salmon had not yet arrived, so they continued down river to meet them, a distance of 70 miles. This meant they didn't get back to the two worried captains until June 2nd. They had with them 7 big fat salmon, which reportedly fried in their own fat.

The weather had been warm, so they thought on June 10th that the snow on the mountains had melted sufficiently to make the passage. They left Long Camp, and went eastward and up the three mile hill, according to the journals, to the plains. (it was a seven mile long hill when we drove up it in 1996) Then they proceeded on to Weippe prairie, where they had first met the Nez Perce the fall before, in September 1805. There they camped until the 15th, when they proceeded on again in pouring rain over slippery roads for 22 miles, to a point about 10 miles past Lolo Creek. (The Lolo Creek in Idaho.) They made 15 miles on the 16th, but were getting into patches of snow 3 feet deep, then later in the day it was 8 feet deep, and it was difficult to find the road. They camped near Hungry Creek.

June 17 was their day of retreat. After leaving the creek and climbing 3 miles up a mountain, still following the road, they found snow over 12 feet deep. They knew there wouldn't be grass for the horses for at least 5 days, so they built a scaffold to store most of their baggage, and went back down to Hungry Creek and camped.

Drewyer and Shannon were sent the next day, to the Indians, to get guides, offering rifles as an inducement to lead as far as the great falls of the Missouri. As the Corps retreated further that day, Colter and his horse fell into the creek, and rolled over and over down the rocky current. No serious injury. Potts, however cut himself accidentally in one of the veins of his leg, and Lewis had a hard time stopping the blood flow. He had to use a tight bandage with a cushion of wood under it. That night they all got back to Lolo Creek and camped. On the 21st, they retreated the 22 miles back to Weippe prairie.

Drewyer got back on the 23rd with the necessary guides so they left Weippe prairie for the last time on the 24th. The first two days got them back to Hungry Creek, and on the 26th, early in the day, they picked up the baggage which they had left on the scaffold nine days before. At that time they had marked the snow level on a tree, and now it had melted almost 4 feet, and was only 7 feet deep. Their guides said that it was a considerable distance to the next place, where there was grass for the horses, and urged them on for the rest of the day. The guides had 3 horses apiece, the Corps had only 2 each. Lewis doubted that they would ever have been able to make the trip without such competent guides.

On the 27th they went 28 miles, passed the Indians Smoking Place, where they all had a smoke, and got to the September 16th encampment of last fall. There was little grass for the horses, but the men had boiled roots and bears oil. After going only 13 miles the next day, however, the horses got plenty of grass at noon and they stayed there for the rest of the day.

They passed the last of the snow on June 29th, went over the dividing ridge (Lolo Pass, not the Continental Divide) before noon, and hit Lolo Creek, the one flowing eastward in Montana. They descended to Lolo Hot Springs for overnight, where they bathed and played in the warm water. When we camped at Lolo Hot Springs on June 18th (1996) it was snowing, so we didn't feel like walking to the springs to play like they did.

The next day, as they descended toward the Bitterroot River and their old Traveler's Rest Camp, Sheilds got two deer and Drewyer got 3, so it was nice to start eating well again. At this camp near Lolo, Montana the captains worked on their final plans to separate, so that each could explore a different part of the country. Lewis was to take a northern route and Clark would take a southern one.

Chapter 9

SEPARATION AT TRAVELER'S REST
July 3, 1806

LEWIS HEADS NORTHWEST — CLARK SOUTHWARD

The captains felt that their expedition would not be complete if they went home without finding answers to two questions; 1.) if the Louisiana Purchase included land that was watered by the Missouri River, how far north did its tributaries go? And 2.), where did the Yellowstone River go?

They knew from the observations they had taken the year before, that the Missouri River at the great falls could be reached much sooner if they all went northeast, rather than follow their old trail to the south. The trouble was that their canoes were cached more than 140 miles south of them. Their plans were for Clark to go south with 50 horses and 23 people, to both pick up the canoes, and explore the Yellowstone. His group of 23 were to split again at Three Forks, into 10 with the canoes to join Lewis, and the rest overland on horses to the Yellowstone. Lewis was to go directly overland from Traveler's Rest to the Missouri at the great falls with his group of 10 to get the portage equipment ready for the canoes when they arrived. Then he would leave some of his group at the river to work on the portage wagons, while he took the rest north to explore the northern extremity of the Marias River.

This was a complicated plan but probably the only way all requirements could be accomplished. But it is inconceivable to me that they would dare such a risky plan. They were 2 or 3 thousand miles from civilization in a possibly hostile environment, going through territory controlled by Crow and Blackfoot Indian tribes that they hadn't been in contact with yet. The probability of getting back home safe was getting greater every day if they stuck together. Splitting into groups of about ten men doesn't seem to me like a very safe way to go. What courage! I have read in history of other examples of courage, where men attacked machine gun nests, or entered burning buildings to save people, but always a rush of adrenalin gave the support to their nervous systems to do the job. But in this case, the Corps of Discovery had no immediate threat to cause adrenalin to flow. They just had deep seated courage and confidence in themselves.

When Lena and I, coming from the west, got to Traveler's Rest at Lolo Montana, we had just come over Route 12, which parallels the old Lolo trail, for we were trying to follow the trail all the way to St. Louis. But when the trail splits and goes hundreds of miles apart, it poses a problem for two people in one van. We had already been down the Yellowstone on another trip, but we hadn't seen the part of the trail that goes through Big Hole Canyon in south Montana, nor had we seen the northern trail that Lewis took to Great Falls, Montana. So we just had to make a big figure eight loop and see it all. We headed south first and then went back to Missoula to get on the scenic northern route. We were well rewarded by the scenery and the historical sites along the way.

So the Corps of Discovery made the separation at 8 am on July 3rd, 1806, Lewis going 5 miles north down the Bitterroot River, then 2 miles north down the Clarks Fork River, probably passing close to present day Missoula. He crossed to the east side, and went 7 miles south, back up the Clarks Fork River, going right through where the city is now. On that day Clark went south 36 miles up the west side of the Bitterroot River before camping.

OVER THE CONTINENTAL DIVIDE

Lewis's 5 Indian guides left him on the 4th, in an emotional goodbye. The pessimistic Indians were confident that the Blackfoot Indians would cut off Lewis's party, and were concerned about their well being. The Nez Perce greatly feared the warlike Blackfoot, and all the tribes that lived in the north country where Lewis was headed in northern Montana and Canada. Lewis gave them plenty of gifts as payment for their guiding service. Before they left they pointed Lewis on the right road, and described the way to the falls of the Missouri. That day Lewis, with Sgt Gass, Drewyer, Joe and Reuben Fields, Frazer, Goodrich, McNeil, Thompson, Werner, and his dog, Seaman, traveled 13 miles, well on the way eastward up the Blackfoot River.

Clark celebrated the 4th of July on the Bitterroot River, a little south of Hamilton, Montana. They made 30 miles that day, spending some time looking for a good place to cross the river. They camped well south of today's Darby. The next day, Colter and Shannon found a suitable ford to get them to the east side, but the current was so swift that some of Clarks specimens got wet when water went over the back of the horse carrying it. After drying them, they proceeded on to Ross's hole near where they had met the Flathead Indians the year before. This is near Sula, Montana.

Clark went over the Continental Divide (at Gibbons Pass) early on July 6, 1806, after 95 miles travel from Traveler's Rest, and Lewis, far to the north, went over the divide (at Lewis and Clark Pass) the afternoon of the next day, after traveling a total of 110 miles. Then they were both back in U.S. territory, after about 11 months absence.

The Blackfoot River that Lewis's horse trail had been following on July 4th, 5th, and 6th for about 90 miles, is now a river well known for float trips. Some sections of the river are

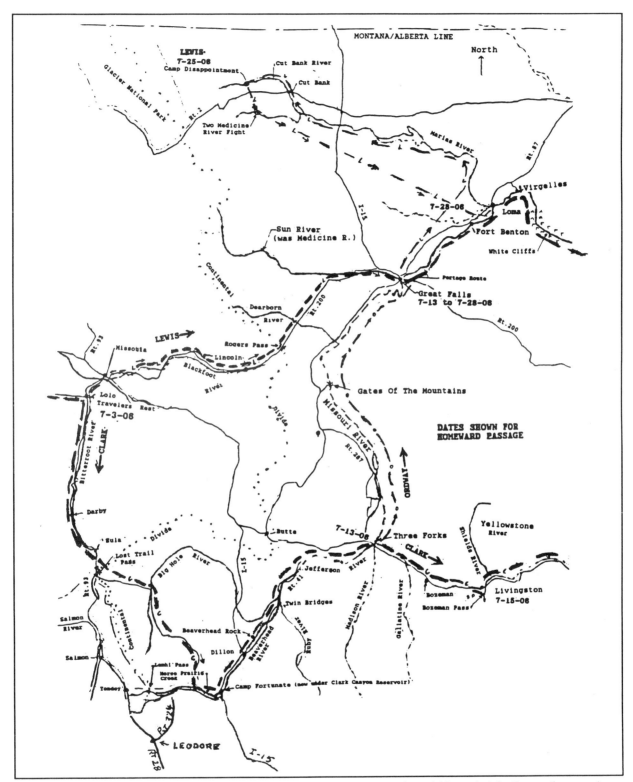

Map 16: Mid-summer and the Corps divides to cover more territory. Lewis and his party take the northern route and explore the Marias River while Clark's party explores the Jefferson and Yellowstone Rivers.

for family floats but some sections are marked as rougher and not for beginners. On the morning of the 7th, Lewis reported a level beautiful plain on the north side of the river. Apparently others have felt the same about the plain, which looked like a lovely valley to us too, for now the town of Lincoln, Montana, is located there, and it is still a beautiful plain. Lincoln is the most prominent town on Highway 200 between Missoula and Great Falls. The divide is only 16 miles east of Lincoln, so Lewis went over that day.

CLARK TO CAMP FORTUNATE

Right after Clark went over the divide and entered a plain on the southeast side, Sacagawea informed him that she knew the place well and that the creek they were following was a branch of the Big Hole River. (This was probably the same spot where Chief Joseph of the Nez Perce camped when they were surprised by the U.S. Army on August 9, 1877. It was called Big Hole Battlefield.) She pointed out to him that, "when we assended the higher part of the plain we would discover a gap in the mountains in our direction to the Canoes, and when we arived at that gap we would See a high point of a mountain covered with snow in our direction to the canoes." This would be the Camp Fortunate where she and the party met her brother Cameahwait in the previous August. She was correct, and they arrived there two days later.

Clark had 9 of his horses stolen on July 7th by Indians that must have been watching them. Not able to catch the thieves, they proceeded on to the hot springs that are now near Jackson on Route 278, through pretty country that now has hay fields as far as you can see. The hay raised in this country is known to be very rich and is good for fattening cattle. They camped here and got to their canoes the next day at Camp Fortunate, now called Clark Canyon Reservoir.

When they were approaching their canoes and the baggage cache at Camp Fortunate on July 8th, the men that used tobacco seemed to have a nicotine attack. This is how Clark put it, "most of the Party with me being Chewers of Tobacco become So impatient to be chewing it that they Scarcely gave themselves time to take their Saddles off their horses before they were off to the deposit." My, wouldn't today's lawyers involved in the tobacco cases have loved to have been there to study those men that had been deprived of their favorite substance for almost a year. There would have been enough scientific studies and legal interviews to make an army of lawyers wealthy, and talk show hosts would have them on every program. As it was, they found most everything in the cache in good condition. Clark gave each chewer two feet off a roll, and then divided the rest into thirds, some for Lewis's group, and the rest for the two groups that would be splitting at Three Forks. (I didn't say spitting). He was a fair officer and the men knew it.

They took one day to dry the canoes, apportion the baggage between horses and canoes, and prepare for leaving early the next morning. On that day "The Squar" (Sacagawea) brought him plants to eat that resembled carrots. Also Sheilds and Collins each got a deer to take with them. That night it was so cold that water in a basin froze 3/4 of an inch thick. Some weather for July 10th!

LEWIS TO GREAT FALLS

Lewis, meanwhile, 180 miles north of Clark, passed the present day Dearborn River and Haystack Butte, and got to the Sun River on July 8th, which flows into the Missouri just above the great falls. They still had three days to go, however, before reaching a point across from their old White Bear Island upper portage camp, which they reached on July 11th.

When Lena and I were driving down Route 200, and could look north and see Haystack Butte, we came around a bend and saw the cattle bunched together that I referred to in connection with the Corps' horses at Long Camp. The cattlemen were from the Broken "O" Ranch and they sure knew animal psychology. Foreman Bruce Fuller had his two sons, Jesse and Steve there, on horses, learning the business. It was truly a sight, to see so many cattle in one bunch.

To get across the Missouri River, Lewis had to have two boats made, one of which they made similar to the round boats that the Mandan women had. They shot some large buffalo bulls for the skins to be used to cover a web of small sticks tied together. These boats, finished on July 12th, worked well the next day, to get them and their baggage across to the southeast side. At this place, they had left a cache full of goods the summer before, at what they called the upper portage camp. Unfortunately, much of the stuff in the cache had been ruined when the river had risen extra high in the spring.

For 3 days, Lewis was worried about where Drewyer was. He had been sent, on the 12th to get seven horses that they couldn't find and they feared were stolen. He had gone back the trail as far as the Dearborn River, and found that the horses were with a large group of Indians and he couldn't do anything to get them back. Lewis had about decided to go up the trail looking for him. He was worried that a bear had attacked him. He had good reason to worry about bears, for on July 10th, he wrote what some of the men reported to him, "they informed us that they had seen a very large bear in the plains which had persued Sergt. Gass and Thomson some distance but their horses enabled them to keep out of it's reach. they were afraid to fire on the bear least their horses would throw them as they were unaccustomed to the gun." Drewyer, however, was about the most competent man of the Corps at survival in the wild. He got back to camp in good condition on July 15th.

McNeal, on July 15th, was sent on horseback to the lower portage camp to see if their cache there had survived the past year. He only got to Willow Run, when a bear attacked and his horse threw him almost under the bear. All he could do was hit the bear with his gun, bending the gun severely, and then climb a tree quickly. He must have given the bear quite a whack for it was stunned and could only shake his head for a moment. So McNeal spent the rest of the day waiting for the bear to go away. When the bear left, he came down from the tree, caught his horse, and returned to camp. Another miracle in the Corps' many encounters with grizzlies.

CLARK TO THREE FORKS

After Clark's party left Camp Fortunate on July 10th, paddling down the Beaverhead River with the horses heading in the same direction, they traveled fast, for they passed present day Dillon about noon. It took both boats and horses two days to reach the Big Hole and the Ruby Rivers, at present day Twin Bridges, but it had taken 11 days on the way upriver the year before. They found out the first day that the boats could go at least as fast as the horses, so they took some of the horse's load and put it in the boats so they could all arrive at Three Forks together. This worked, and the horses got there only an hour ahead of the boats at noon on July 13th. This four day trip had taken 19 days when going upriver a year before. Three Forks, the beginning of the Missouri River, was the place where the second major separation of the Corps was planned.

Besides the Charbonneau family, Clark had 20 men which would be divided about in half, 10 continuing down the Missouri under the command of Sgt. Ordway to join Lewis; the rest with Clark, on horses, across country to find the upper reaches of the Yellowstone River, and proceed down that river to it's end where it enters the Missouri. Instead of wasting any time, after lunch on the 13th, the horses swam to the east side of the Gallatin River, were loaded, and they headed southeastward toward a gap in the mountains. Clark ends his diary for July 13 with: "The Indian woman who has been of great Service to me as a pilot through this Country recommends a gap in the mountain more South which I shall cross."

This day, July 13th was the same day that Lewis reached the upper portage camp at the head of the great falls. It had been just 10 days since they both left Traveler's Rest.

ORDWAY TO GREAT FALLS

The only record that exists of Ordway's 6 day canoe trip down the Missouri to meet Lewis, is in Ordway's diary. He had with him Colter, Collins, Cruzat, Howard, LePage, Potts, Whitehouse, Willard, and Wiser. They had 6 canoes, which were more than adequate to carry what little baggage they had left, but they knew they would pick up more from the 2 caches downstream. Six canoes for ten men, must have been difficult, for that left two canoes to be manned by a single paddler. Collins apparently was one that had one all to himself, for he did not return to the camp on the night of the 14th. The next day he sure had luck at hunting, for he shot 3 deer before 9 am, then a fat buck, and four elk later in the day. In the next 3 days he killed a beaver, a fawn elk, 2 mountain sheep, and 3 more deer. Colter and Cruzat were killing animals all along too and I wondered what 10 men would do with so many animals. I found out when I read of their activities at the White Bear Island camp. They were treating the skins to make clothes. (They couldn't find a K Mart anyplace). Their rugged life must have worn out clothes pretty fast. The mountain sheep skin and bones were only to take back as specimens for President Jefferson.

ORDWAY AND GASS OVER THE PORTAGE

Ordway passed through the Gates of the Mountains on July 16th, and met up with Gass and party at the upper portage camp (Great Falls) on July 19th. Lewis had already left Gass and his 5 men, three days before, and had headed for the Marias River with Drewyer and the Fields brothers. The Ordway and Gass diaries both tell of the activities of these 16 men for the next 9 days, until July 28th, when the lucky (miracle?) meeting with Lewis took place.

Sgt Gass and crew had been working on the portage wagons since they had been there at the upper portage camp, and were ready to see if the horses could pull them on the evening of July 20th. They hitched up the four horses to the new wagon tongues and found that they would draw all right, which was encouraging. But the horses were covered with mosquitos and small flies, which tormented them. The next morning the horses were gone, and I can't say that I blame them. Hunting for them all day was unsuccessful, so the men started to draw the wagons with the canoes on them by themselves. They also gathered dry buffalo dung and made fires to smoke the mosquitos away. On the 22nd they found the horses, hitched them up, and set out with 2 canoes, but then the wagon broke down after 5 miles. They fixed that and then moved along with 2 more canoes.

Their burdens were not helped by two occurrences on the 23rd. Wiser cut his leg with a knife so bad that he couldn't walk, and then it began raining and hailing. They did get 2 canoes as far as Willow Run. (now Box Elder Coulee). This is where they had the bad hail storm a year before that hurt them all so bad and held them up for a couple days. Willow Run had flooded so deep at that time that they couldn't get across. It had probably flooded again. This time they left the canoes there and the next day went back to the head of the portage for 2 more canoes. They tried to get the largest canoe moving but it was too heavy and they left it there permanently. They really didn't need it because they found the white pirogue at the lower camp in good condition.

When reading about their activities for the next 3 days (24th to the 26th), I sure had to admire the men's ability to keep going in spite of obstacles. The rain made the plains muddy and they had to slop through it with wooden wheeled wagons that hardly took the weight of the canoes. There were swollen streams to cross. Some slept under overturned boats on the night of the 25th, but the ground was covered with water and it just flowed under and around them as they lay there. Others sat up and tried to keep a fire burning in the rain. But when anyone works so hard all day, there isn't any trouble sleeping. I can see them getting up in the morning and letting the water drip from their clothes, then wolfing down a breakfast of buffalo or badger that Collins had killed the day before. Every one of those men were an example in persistence for all of us today. Those 3 days they got all the canoes from Willow Run to the Portage Creek. (Now Belt Creek.)

Colter and Potts (you should read about these two in later history, [see the sign at Three Forks for a brief outline]) kept busy shooting the canoes down the rapids to the cache a mile below Portage Creek where the white pirogue had been stored for a year. This place was called the lower portage camp when they were on the way upriver, because the baggage had been taken out of the canoes there.

So, on the night of July 27, 1806 the portage was complete, and the next day the horses swam to the north side of the Missouri for Gass and Willard to take them to the Marias River confluence, and the pirogue and 5 canoes pushed off, headed for the same place.

While I read the Journals about the great falls portage, both on the way upriver in 1805 and down river in 1806, I wondered where the Blackfoot and Crow Indians were while the explorers were there. The Corps was never bothered by a single Indian. It couldn't be because there was no game in that vicinity. There were big herds of buffalo and the explorers shot elk for their experimental boat. I wonder if the large number of grizzlies around the falls were keeping the Indians away. Indian hunters could get all the game they wanted elsewhere, so why should they try to interfere with those fierce creatures? Bears gave the explorers plenty of trouble, but not as much as if unfriendly or thieving Indians were pestering them as they pulled those clumsy wagons, and had supplies in several places. Maybe those bears actually helped them! Just a guess.

Chapter 10

LEWIS TO CAMP DISAPPOINTMENT

Lewis had been bitterly disappointed the year before, at the upper portage camp on July 9, 1805, when he realized that his metal boat was a failure. He had another disappointment coming up, on his excursion up the Marias River to discover the most northerly area drained by the Missouri River.

He, Drewyer, and Reubin and Joseph Field left the upper portage camp on July 16th. Drewyer and Reubin Field swam the horses across to the north side of the Missouri above the White Bear Islands, and then had to swim them across the Sun River to get on it's east side. Lewis and Joe Field loaded their baggage in the 2 skin boats and joined the other two. Then, after loading the baggage on the horses, they set out for Rainbow Falls, and then the Great Falls in order for Lewis to make more sketches and measurements of the falls.

The next 2 days they went almost due north, camping on the Teton River the first night, and then on the Marias River the next, a distance of 44 miles. The next 3 days they went up the Marias on a northwest course to present day Cut Bank, a distance of over 70 miles. They had passed the site of present day Tiber Dam and its reservoir, and then, on the 21st, the forks which were the mouths of the Medicine and Cut Bank Creeks. He chose to follow the north fork, the Cut Bank, because the waters were clearer, which indicated to him that it came from the mountains. He was beginning to doubt that these waters came from as far north as he had hoped.

The party continued west on Cut Bank Creek, about 20 miles, to the most northerly point on their entire trip, which was about 24 miles from the present day Canadian border, and about 110 miles north of the men struggling to get the canoes down the portage around the falls. He was about 300 miles from Capt Clark down on the Yellowstone River, who was just passing the mouth of the Bighorn River. Lewis stayed at that camp from July 24th, to the 26th, trying to get Longitude and Latitude for his report to the president. He hoped for clear weather at noon, so he could get the maximum altitude of the sun, but it was cloudy all the time he was there. This was one reason he named the camp Camp Disappointment. Another reason was that he hadn't found the more northerly point of the Louisiana Purchase. He suspected that the Milk River, or another one, were further north, and he was right. Food was scarce while they were there, and their only meat was tainted, so they rendered it, and mixed it with some "meal of cows."(they must have been saving the "cows" all the way from Idaho over a month before). He sent Drewyer and Joe Fields down about 10 miles to where the Two Medicine Creek was, to see if there was any game there. They came back with a buck, so they ate well again.

The clouds hadn't cleared by 9 am on July 26th, so they gave up and headed southeast, and had lunch on the banks of the Two Medicine Creek. While there, he wrote about seeing three different specimens of the Cottonwood that are seldom seen together, one of them from the western side of the Rocky Mountains. After eating, they continued down river 3 miles, when Lewis had Drewyer stay along the river while he and the other two ascended the bluffs to the plain. That's where he saw the Piegan Indians, a member of the fierce Blackfoot tribe.

THE TWO MEDICINE FIGHT

When looking through his spyglass, Lewis counted 30 horses, and planned on big trouble. The Blackfoot nation was friendly with the British, but enemies of anyone else that came into their territory, which is now western Montana and Alberta. He knew that if he tried to run away it would be futile, so he decided to take the friendly approach, as he had done with all tribes before. The Indians hadn't seen him because they were looking down towards the river at Drewyer. When they saw Lewis slowly advancing toward them with Joe Field displaying the American Flag, they "appeared to run about in a very confused manner as if much alarmed." Then one of them mounted his horse and ran full speed toward them. Lewis dismounted and held out his hand. This made the Indian run just as fast back to his party. Then they all advanced on horseback toward Lewis and the two Fields brothers. Lewis walked forward, and shook hands with the first one, and then passed on to shake with the rest.

The Indians asked to smoke, but Lewis said that Drewyer had the pipe, and proposed that one of their men and Reuben Fields go looking for him. Lewis then gave a medal, a flag, and a handkerchief to the 3 Indians who were supposed to be chiefs. There were only 8 Indians, even though they had 30 horses, and they seemed agitated and surprised by this accidental meeting. Lewis proposed that they camp together down on the river.

On the way down they met Drewyer, Reuben Fields, and the Indian; they then picked a spot side of the river for a camp and a smoke. The spot selected was, according to Lewis, in a bottom where "their bluffs being so steep it is impossible to ascend them; in this bottom there stand three solitary trees near one of which the Indians formed a large semicircular camp of dressed buffalo skins and invited us to partake of their shelter which Drewyer and myself accepted and the Fieldses lay near the fire in front of the sheter."

In 1964, a search for this exact campsite was made, and three very old cottonwood trees were discovered, right where the camp was supposed to have been. They might, or they might not have been the same trees.

When we were in Cut Bank and Browning in 1996, a trip to the site wasn't possible because the whole area was under water from a recent flood. We hope anyone reading this will have better timing when trying to visit the site. There is a very interesting museum in Cut Bank that has up to date information about the Two Medicine Fight Site. Also in Cut Bank, is County Attorney Larry Epstein, who spoke to our Foundation. His knowledge of the incident and the site is phenomenal.

Before sleeping with the Indians that night of July 26th, 1806, Lewis had a long talk with them with the help of Drewyer as interpreter. He told them that he had come to urge them to make peace with their neighbors, and that he had told all nations to come and trade with him. He said he had left his party at the falls of the Missouri, and was on his way to meet them at the mouth of the Marias River. Then they told him that they were part of a large band, now located 1/2 day from them on their way to the mouth of the Marias River. This made Lewis alarmed about the safety of his main party down at the portage. He really wanted to get away in a hurry, but diplomatically proposed that if they would all go down to the Missouri together he would give them tobacco and ten horses. He had 6 horses, and the portage party had 4, that would not be needed when they got into the canoes.

Lewis alerted the men that the Indians would try to steal their horses in the night, and provided for an all night watch. He took the first watch and then he roused Reubin Field for the next one at 11:30.

The next morning at daylight, the Indian that had received the medal, quickly grabbed up both of the Fields brothers guns and ran with them. At the same time two others snatched the guns of Drewyer and Lewis. It looked bad, but do you remember who were the fastest runners in the Corps when they raced with the Nez Perce at Long camp? Drewyer and Reuben Fields. Even though Reubin was asleep when his brother alerted him, and the Indian had a good start, Reubin caught him at 60 paces, and stabbed him through the heart. The two brothers got their guns back.

When Drewyer saw an Indian grabbing his gun he quickly wrestled with him and got it. This scuffle awakened Lewis, who saw another Indian running off with his own gun. He ran after him with his pistol, hollering at him to lay it down. He dropped it at once, but at the same time the Fields came back with their guns and asked permission to shoot him. Lewis refused, because the man didn't seem to want to kill them. But Lewis did tell his men to fire on any Indian attempting to run off their horses, which they were doing. When he saw his horse being driven up a niche in the bluffs, he shot the thief through the belly. The Indian shot back, barely missing Lewis's head, and he could hear the wind of the bullet. The rest of the Indians ran away.

All four men, with no wounds, and all their guns intact, collected the horses, saddled up, and left. They took with them one of the Indians guns, the U.S. flag that they had given to one Indian, and some of the Indian's buffalo meat. The medal that was around the neck of the dead one was left with the body.

Lewis figured that the Indians would pursue them, or at least alert their larger party who were headed for the mouth of the Marias River. It was necessary to get there first, so they traveled as fast as possible, making 63 miles by 3 pm, when they reached the Teton River. After stopping there for 1 1/2 hours, they proceeded on for another 17 miles, when they took a two hour rest stop. They killed a buffalo for something to eat, and set out again, leisurely, in the moonlight, until 2 am, when they stopped to sleep until morning. This, the 27th of July, had been one tough day.

The next morning, July 28th, they were all so sore they could hardly stand up, but they set out at daybreak. After 12 miles, they were close to the Missouri when they heard a gunshot; then at 8 miles further, they heard more shots coming from the river, which made them rejoice.

Then, Lewis writes, "on arriving at the bank of the river had the unspeakable satisfaction to see our canoes coming down." Ordway and party had left the lower portage that morning, and were just passing by. What a coincidence! This was near present day Fort Benton and they were back with two thirds of the Corps of Discovery. The other third, of course, was with Clark, over 200 miles southeast of them on the Yellowstone River.

ON TO THE YELLOWSTONE CONFLUENCE

Lewis stripped the horses, giving them "a final discharge" and got into the boats, quickly. They still didn't want to be attacked by the Blackfoot, who they thought would come for revenge. They proceeded to the cache at the Marias confluence. They found almost all of the deposits in good condition, except the red pirogue, which was too rotten to use. Gass and Willard, who were bringing the horses from the portage, were supposed to be there before the rest, but didn't arrive until they were all ready to proceed on down the Missouri. They all descended 15 miles and camped on the south bank, in case the Blackfoot attacked from the north.

Early the next day, July 29th, Lewis sent the Field brothers in one canoe, and Colter and Collins in another, out ahead to hunt, and they all proceeded rapidly down river. They passed the White Cliffs and camped in the same site that they'd had on May 29, 1805, over a year before. On August 1st, after they had gone almost 250 river miles in 4 days, they camped below the Musselshell River, now part of Fort Peck Lake. This had taken 14 days on the way upriver. They stayed the next day to dry their baggage and skins from the 30 or so animals that they had recently shot, which needed to be preserved. They proceeded on, on the morning of August 3rd, and passed the canoe of Colter and Collins who were on shore hunting. The men in the boats hailed as they went by, but heard no answer. Colter and

Collins wouldn't be seen again for another 9 days.

By the next evening they had passed the Big Dry and the Milk Rivers. Ordway and Willard had been hunting in a small canoe and didn't get to camp until about midnight. The current had driven them into a fallen tree called a sawyer, which threw Willard overboard. Ordway stayed with the canoe but was driven down river until he got the canoe to shore, then returned by land to try to rescue Willard. Willard got some sticks together for buoyancy, and set himself free from the sawyers. Then Ordway got the canoe and rescued him. If Willard had not been a strong swimmer he would have been drowned. This all happened in the dark.

All went well for the next 3 days and they reached the mouth of the Yellowstone on August 7, 1806, at 4 pm. Lewis found fragments of Clark's note, enough to realize that he had proceeded on, and he noticed how bad the mosquitos were. He left a note for Colter and Collins, in case they were behind. He had worried about them since August 3rd, but didn't know if they were ahead or behind him. Then he continued down because he figured Clark would be camping a short distance down river.

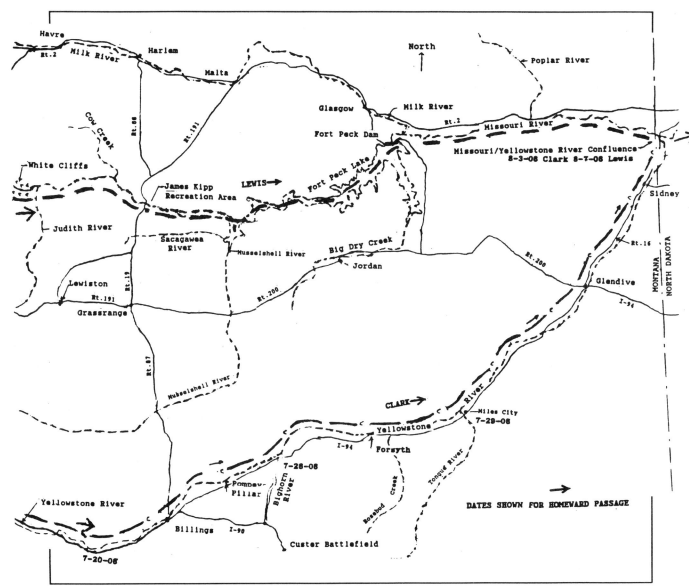

Map 17: Homeward Passage, the separate exploring parties reunite first part of August, 1806.

Chapter 11

CLARK DOWN THE YELLOWSTONE

Back at Three Forks on July 13th, Clark and party left Ordway at five o'clock in the afternoon and headed for the Yellowstone River. He had with him Sgt. Pryor, Shields, Shannon, Bratton, LaBiche, Windsor, Hall, Gibson, York, Charbonneau, Sacagawea, and Pomp. He also had 49 horses and a colt.

They followed along the Gallatin River the next morning, following it upriver wherever they could, but there were so many beaver dams that made the going difficult they had to go up onto the plains to make any progress. They saw plenty of elk, deer, and antelope, but little sign of buffalo. Sacagawea explained to him why the buffalo were not in that hilly area. Years before, there had been plenty of buffalo, even up to the head of the Jefferson River, but that was before the Crows and Blackfoot got so powerful, (from the acquisition of guns) and would kill anyone caught on the buffalo plains. So the Shoshonees were afraid of leaving the protection of the mountains, except for quick trips to kill a few buffalo and return immediately. Most of their hunting was in these hills, so the buffalo soon became depleted. In those days there weren't any game wardens to prevent the depletion of game populations. The Indians usually were pretty good at preserving their resources, so this situation is surprising.

That night, the 14th, they camped east of present day Bozeman, Montana, and the next day went over the Bozeman Pass, which separates the waters of the Missouri and Yellowstone Rivers. It was then about 9 miles downhill to the Yellowstone, which they reached at 2 pm on the 15th. They rested for 3 hours and were off again for 9 miles, following the river, to camp near the Shields River.

The stones and gravel were so rough it wore out the hoofs of the horses and their feet were getting sore. Clark had Shannon kill a fat bull buffalo, so they could use the skin to make shoes for the horses. These seemed to relieve the horses considerably and the party could proceed on.

Their first five days (15th through 19th) going down the Yellowstone, was on horseback, and they had traveled 115 miles by Clark's estimates, but all the while they were looking for trees large enough to make canoes. They passed two Indians forts, a reminder that the Indian wars were going on; then smoke signals were seen on the 18th. Clark made notes of every creek or river that entered the Yellowstone, and the geography as it continually changed.

On the 18th, two incidents made building boats more necessary. Charbonneau's horse stepped into a badger hole while chasing a buffalo and was "a good deal brused on his hip sholder & face". Then Gibson, while attempting to mount his horse after shooting a deer, fell on an inch diameter snag, and drove it two inches into the muscular part of his thigh. This was a terribly painful wound which effected his knee, hip, and thigh. Clark dressed the wound and made a specially padded blanket for his saddle, so he could proceed. After 9 miles on the 19th, Gibson could stand it no longer. They stopped to let him rest, and sent Shields into a wooded river bottom to look for acceptable trees, for they had to get Gibson into a boat. Shields came out of the woods, chased by a two bears. He had shot two deer while he was there.

Poor Gibson was obliged to travel on another 2 1/2 hours in pain. Then Clark put him under the shade of a tree, with Pryor to take care of him, and proceeded on, looking for large trees.

That evening, 4 miles further down river, Clark set up camp where there was good grazing near some trees, that might do to make boats. Then he and Shields rode further down to look for better ones. When he returned, Pryor and Gibson had arrived at the new camp. The next morning he sent Pryor and Shields off looking for better trees, but they returned unsuccessful. So he made the decision to make two canoes right there, and lash them together for stability. Then Gibson wouldn't be subjected to the pain of riding a horse any more. Clark sure had compassion. That day, the 20th, the men worked until dark getting the trees ready.

Half of their horses were missing the next morning, stolen by Indians. It is ironic that it was the same morning that Ordway and Gass were missing their horses up at the Great Falls portage. But where the portage crew would find theirs, Clark's were gone for good. The other half of his horses had run into the woods, so they found them.

PRYOR LEAVES FOR MANDAN VILLAGE

On the evening of the 23rd, the boats were ready to go, and Clark directed Sgt Pryor to proceed, with the remaining horses, to the Mandan village. He was to deliver to a Mr Heney that lived near there, a letter which asked him to urge some Indians chiefs to be ready to go down to St. Louis with the Corps as they passed through. Pryor was to be accompanied by Shannon and Windsor.

Both parties left at 8 am the next morning, the 24th. They met again six miles below the mouth of the Clark's Fork of the Yellowstone River. Clark, in the boats, stopped to help Pryor get his horses to the south side. But Pryor was having trouble, and needed another man to help him drive the horses. His troubles were real, but they amused me when I read about them. Their horses had been trained by the Nez Perce or Shoshone Indians, who used them to chase animals when hunting, and the horses must have enjoyed the pursuit. So even when they didn't have a rider, and there were animals to chase, the horses did it just the same. Whenever they met up with a herd of buffalo, off they would go to have some fun. Pryor needed another man on a fast horse, to help him chase the buffalo away before the trailing horses could get to them. H. Hall, who could not swim, said he was willing to go with Pryor on the horses. So both parties proceeded on, not meeting again until August 8th. Clark passed the site of present day Billings that day, and traveled a total of 62 river miles.

The next day, the 25th, Clark passed a 200 foot high rock near the south bank of the river. He climbed the rock and engraved his name and the date, July 25, 1806, on the side of the rock. He named the rock Pompy's Tower, in honor of Sacagewea's baby whom he had nicknamed Pomp. At this time Pomp was almost a year and a half old and was probably walking and even jabbering a little. I wonder if he jabbered in Shoshone, French, or English? Eventually he would learn six languages. Can you imagine an active tyke that old, crossing half the continent in a river canoe? I'll bet the whole crew was constantly on the alert to keep him from falling overboard. Besides naming the rock after him, a creek directly opposite from the rock on the north shore, was named "baptiest Creek," after his real first name. It is now Pompeys Pillar Creek. That day Clark chipped out of the face of a rock, a 3 foot long bone of "the rib of a fish," which was actually a dinosaur, to be taken back as a scientific specimen. At night the Corps camped 4 miles down river at the mouth of Shannon Creek, after making 58 river miles (today only about 30 miles by Route I-94) that day. That must have been a busy day.

Pompeys Pillar, east of Billings, Montana.

Lena and I climbed Pompeys Tower in 1985, and, sure enough, Clark's name was there, extremely visible and well preserved. This is an interesting stop for any camper, for other historic events happened there in the days after the Lewis and Clark visit.

Pryor got to Pompeys Pillar too, but not on horses. All his horses were stolen when they got up on the morning of the 26th, just two days after they left Clark. The four of them hiked toward the river and reached it at Pompeys Pillar. Clark had already left, so they were without any form of transportation to get home. They made two round boats from buffalo skins and sticks, just like the Mandan women did, and like Lewis's party had made, two weeks before, to get across the Missouri River. That first night at Pompeys Pillar they were attacked by a wolf while they were sleeping. It first chewed Pryor's hand, then attacked Windsor before Shannon was able to shoot it.

On the next day Clark's party came to the mouth of the Big Horn River, where they camped. Clark and LaBiche explored about 7 miles up this river, finding it 5 to 7 feet deep. This depth made me wonder if the first steam boats couldn't have gone up it some distance. Seventy years later, In 1876, the riverboat Far West, which was reportedly at the mouth of the Big Horn, was loaded with the wounded soldiers from the battle of the Little Big Horn, and rushed them in 56 hours to the hospital at Bismarck, North Dakota. But, if the Big Horn was as deep as Clark said, maybe the boat was able to sail up much closer to the battlefield, which is 50 miles away from the mouth.

On the 27th and 28th, he covered 153 river miles, and passed the Tongue River on the 29th, where Miles City is today. We found that city to be a good stop for campers, with a good campground and a Custer County Fair you won't forget, that is if you get there at the end of August. This is the place to learn all about wheat farming and see farm animals. And, what appears in my diary for that day, was the way I raved about the food, especially the pie ala mode we got in a Methodist Pie Shack!

Before Clark reached the Powder River he went over shoal rapids that required lowering the canoes down by hand. There always seemed to be a rapid before they reached an entering river. Then a violent storm made them draw the canoes out of the water at a dry creek he named after York. They camped opposite the Powder River to get away from its waters, which he said were too warm and too dirty. That night, a gang of buffalo crossing the river endangered their canoes, and disturbed them all night. Nowadays, campers would be thrilled if they could see a gang of buffalo crossing a river.

They were stopped for an hour near Glendive on August 1st for a traffic jam. Large gangs of buffalo were crossing, and there was nothing to do but stop, and let them have the right of way. They shot 4 of them, as their meat was getting spoiled. The next day as they were passing a sand bar, a large bear smelled the meat in the boat and attacked them through the water. Three shots were enough to discourage him and he swam back to shore.

They made good time with that little double hulled boat of their's, and crossed into present day North Dakota on August 2nd; then to the mouth of the Yellowstone at 8 am on August 3rd, 1806. They were going to stay there, and wait for Lewis and party to arrive, but their fiercest enemy attacked again in huge swarms; mosquitos. They stayed overnight, but they were bitten so bad, and baby Pomps face was so swollen, that they had to find a better place to wait for Lewis. They left him a note at the point of the confluence, and headed down the Missouri River to try for a better camp with less mosquitos.

Chapter 12

DOWN THE MISSOURI RIVER

Clark's August 4th camp was no better; the mosquitos drove them out at 4 am. The mosquitos continued to bother them as they went slowly down the river, until the 6th and 7th when the wind blew and it turned cold. This was a "joyfull circumstance to the Party," Clark wrote. Pryor, Shannon, Hall, and Windsor showed up August 8th in the morning, coming down in those round boats, after a 15 day absence. They told their story to Clark about losing the horses and building the bull boats (round skin canoes). Pryor's wound from the wolf had about healed. They were lucky that those two tubs got them the rest of the way down to the Missouri River, which Clark's diary says is over 500 miles. (about half of that as the crow flies) Clark was disappointed that Pryor had lost the horses that would have been used to buy food supplies from the Mandans and Hidatsas. Therefore he figured on getting more animal skins before he got to the villages, to be used for trading. So he sent the hunters out. However, he was glad that the arrival of these four made his party complete. The next thing was to join up with Lewis.

After Lewis left the confluence, seven miles down, they found a camp with meat hanging up, a fresh fire, and a hat that they recognized as belonging to Gibson, but no one was there. I haven't read of any explanation for this empty camp, but Gibson might have lost his hat there as Clark's party passed a few days before. The only explanation I can think of for the fresh fire and no canoe, is that two Indians were there, and ran away when they heard Lewis's canoes arriving. What is your guess?

At 10 am the next day, when 3 miles from the White Earth River, Lewis came to a beach that would be good for drawing out two leaking canoes needing patching, so they halted until the 11th, when they proceeded on.

Clark's crew did a lot of hunting for the next 3 days, and Clark got a chance to finish some of his maps. He camped in the same place on the 9th and 10th, and left a message for Lewis as he left on the 11th. Two Illinois trappers were seen by Clark, at noon on the 11th, the first non-Indians they had seen for a year and a half. These men had spent the last winter with the Teton Sioux and had been robbed. As they were coming upriver the year before, they had passed, at the Kansas River, the keelboat that the captains had sent down from Fort Mandan under Corporal Warfington. This was good news for Clark, to know that the shipment to President Jefferson had got that far. (The Kansas River comes into the Missouri at present day Kansas City.) But the news that the Mandans and Minnetarees were at war with the Arikaras, and that the Assiniboins were at war with the Mandans, wasn't good news to Clark. He thought that he and Lewis had persuaded them all to live at peace with each other.

Lewis's worst day of the trip was August 11th, the day before his party met Clark's. That day they proceeded to the point on the Missouri River that Lewis considered further north than any other point, and he wanted to take noon sights with his sextant. When they got there, it was past noon, so he decided to go shoot some elk. He and Cruzat went ashore to hunt for some. After getting one, they took different routes to get another. The next victim would be Lewis, for he was dressed in brown leather, and one eyed Cruzat mistakenly shot him through the buttocks. A 54 caliber ball went in one side and came out the other, then fell into his trousers. He called out to Cruzat, "damn you, you have shot me," but got no answer. Then he was sure it was an Indians attack, so he ran back to the boat and called the men to arms. With his wounds, he couldn't go with the men, but he got his gun, his airgun, and his pistol, ready to fight to the end. Later the men came back with Cruzat, saying that there were no Indians. Cruzat was alarmed and apologetic, saying it was unintentional.

Gass helped Lewis dress both wounds with "tents of patent lint into the ball holes, the wounds bled considerably but I was hapy to find that it had touched neither bone nor artery," Lewis wrote, in spite of his pain. So they proceeded on down river. They got to the camp that Clark had evacuated that morning, and found a note from Clark telling about Pryor losing the horses, and coming down by skin canoes. Lewis knew that hurt the chance of getting Indian chiefs to accompany them to St. Louis.

TOGETHER AGAIN

August 12, 1806 was the day they all reunited. Before Lewis met Clark, he met the two white hunters from Illinois; Dixon and Hancock, who Clark had seen the day before. Lewis gave them some powder and shot and a file, and then proceeded on. After that, Colter and Collins finally caught up to them after being behind for 9 days. These two had waited several days for Lewis upstream, thinking that they were ahead, then they hurried down to catch up. It was just a little different from Shannon being lost two years before, but probably not quite as distressing. At noontime, when Clark's party stopped for lunch, Lewis finally came to join them.

The jubilation of the meeting was subdued when Clark saw Lewis in the pirogue wounded. Clark dressed his wounds. Lewis predicted that he would be well in 20 or 30 days, and he would live up to it. This day would be the last writing Lewis would do until the end of the journey. He didn't need to, for now he had Captain Clark again. They had been separated for 40 days and had traveled through a land of both beauty and danger, and all had survived.

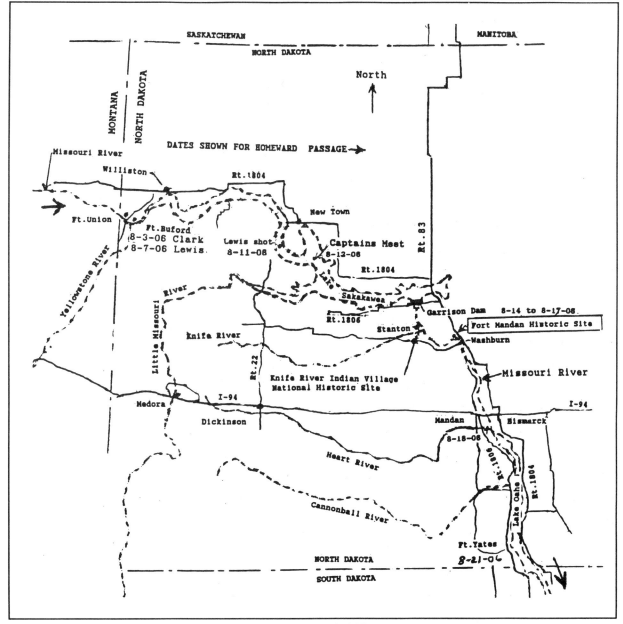

Map 18: Homeward passage, through the Dakotas August of 1806.

At 3 pm that day Dixon and Hancock arrived, having decided to go down with the Corps as far as the Mandans. They all, together again, proceeded on.

The first Indians that Clark had seen since they left the Nez Perce were seen on the river on August 13th. They had come 86 miles, passing the Little Missouri River. The next day they arrived at the Minnetare Indian village, where both the Corps and the Indians shot off their blunderbusses in greeting. They visited Chief Black Moccasin, who was in tears because he had lost his son, who was killed by the Blackfoot Indians. This was the Hidatsa village, part of the Minnetare, (Gros Ventre, Big Belly) tribe.

Then they visited Chief Black Cat at his Mandan village, where the Indians were all well pleased to see them. They ate and smoked with Black Cat. This village was much smaller than it had been when the Corps was there before, because there had been a quarrel in the village and many of the lodges moved across the river.

Clark invited the Hidatsa chiefs and Jessome, the interpreter for the lower Mandan villages, to come and have a council. The purpose of this meeting was to persuade some of the Indians chiefs to go with them to the United States. They figured that if Indians could see the greatness of the white nation, they would more easily conform in trade and defense matters. It was necessary to get influential chiefs to visit, so their importance would lend more weight to what they would be telling their people on their return. Chief Black Cat would have been a good one, but he was afraid the Teton Sioux would kill him on the way through their territory. The Sioux had been at war with them and had killed several of his people. Only one man wanted to go, but he was one that had already stolen Gibson's knife and was known to have a bad character. Clark rejected him and shamed him into giving the knife back, which he did.

Clark set his camp midway between the Hidatsa and Mandans villages, and received gifts of corn and beans from both tribes. His men were busy making themselves clothing from the skins they had collected. But poor Lewis was still in a lot of pain while there. Ordway writes that when Clark was dressing Lewis's wound he fainted for a short time.

Colter had been talking to the two Illinois men about joining them as they went up the Missouri on a trapping expedition. He asked the captains for permission to resign from the party in order to do this. They couldn't give permission if any others would ask to leave, for the safety of the party had to be preserved. However, the rest did not want to leave, and they wished Colter success in his venture. So the captains discharged and paid Colter off, and gave him powder and lead and other articles they didn't need any more. The others gave him gifts and a hearty farewell.

There was another opportunity for a speech to the Hidatsas when Clark presented the swivel cannon to them. This cannon was of no use to the Corps because the pirogue wouldn't handle the discharge, and would be an extra load if they took it back to St. Louis. They had a big ceremony, and Clark scolded them for following the Corps the year before, and attacking the Shoshone Indians after his back was turned. He said this was bad because he had just shaken the hand of the Shoshones, and told them that the Hidatsas had said they would be peaceful with them. Maybe it was on this trip to fight the Shoshones that Black Moccasin's son was killed by the Blackfoot. After Clark's speech, the swivel was fired, and it was presented to the Hidatsa.

They finally got a chief to go down river with them. Chief Big White, or Sheheke, agreed to go, if his wife and son, and Jessome's wife and two children could go also. The captains agreed, and set the men at the task of fastening two large canoes together to make them more stable for the two families.

They were ready to proceed on down river from the Mandans on August 17, 1806. Charbonneau, Sacagawea, and Pomp would not be going to St. Louis with them. They paid him off, $500.33, which was for a horse and his leather lodge, which they had taken upriver with them. His salary had been probably something like $25 per month for his services. The money was for Charbonneau; nothing for Sacagawea, even though he was really hired because of her. That was standard practice in those days, which was an injustice that most people took for granted, even most women. Thankfully, women don't take it for granted any more. Clark offered to take them all down with him, but Charbonneau refused, because there would be no employment as an interpreter. Clark even offered to provide an education for Pomp, but the kid was still nursing and couldn't leave its mother. Charbonneau did say that he would take him down in a year if Clark would raise him in a manner which Clark thought proper. I think it must have been hard for Clark, and the rest of the men likewise, to say goodby to the much admired Sacagawea, and especially little Pomp, who had been with them since birth.

The boats went down a half mile to where Big White's Mandan village was, and Clark walked to the chiefs lodge to pick them up. All the chief's friends were sitting around smoking, and the women were crying. It was as if the chief and family were going to die. It really must have been heart rending for them, to leave from the only place they have ever known, to a far-off country that none of them had ever seen, and to a strange way of living. Clark had another chance to talk to the ones remaining about peace, and told them that he would talk to the Arikaras when he passed their village, to tell them to talk peace with the Mandans. Clark smoked with them, gave them some powder and lead, and then walked with the whole company down to the boats.

Next they visited Fort Mandan, which they had built the first winter of their expedition, and found that most of it had been burned by accident. Only one of the cabins was standing and some of the pickets in the front. (A few years after that, the site itself was gone, because the river wore it away as it changed its course.) Then they proceeded on to an old Arikara village and camped, making 18 miles that day.

Big White told stories on the way down to the Heart River, as they passed sites where the Mandans had formerly lived. This was before they retreated north to get away from the Teton Sioux. Their camp that night of August 18th was where Fort Lincoln Park is now, which has rebuilt the earth lodges that Big White told about. He had been born in that vicinity.

Big White also told an old Indians tale about the origin of the Mandans. There was originally a large village below the earth, and a grapevine grew up to the surface, allowing the village to see light. Then they all climbed up the grapevine to the surface. Now the

Mandans believe that when they die, they will return to the village below. Other Indians tribes have other tales about the origin of things, and they are so interesting when properly told. None of these tales are told as though they care whether anyone believes it or not, just a traditional story that pleases the imagination. I truly enjoy listening to them.

"Capt. Lewis'ses wounds are heeling very fast, I am much in hope of his being able to walk in 8 or 10 days," Clark wrote, on August 19. They only went 10 miles that day because of high winds and rain. The next day they passed the Cannonball River at noon, and got into present South Dakota before they camped, having gone 81 miles. Their little fleet was doing good. It consisted of the white pirogue, two catamarans, (canoes lashed together) and three single canoes. There were 36 in the party, including 3 children.

Two of the men that had been with the Corps of Discovery on their way upriver in 1804, were seen on the river on August 21st. They had helped Warfington take the barge back to St. Louis. They were now on their way back up to the Mandans, and told the captains about 700 Sioux that were on their way up to fight with the Mandans and Hidatsas. If so, that would be the end of tribal peace for a while, at least with the Sioux. These two men had a young fellow with them that wanted to quit, and go back down with the Corps. The captains agreed and gave him an oar to help them paddle.

Clark had promised the Mandans that he would try, when he passed the Arikara villages, to talk them into being peaceful with the Mandans. There had been fights between them this past winter. in which some had been killed. The Arikaras were near where Mobridge, South Dakota. is now, and the Corps received a nice welcome from the first village. Clark sat down, with Big White close by his side, and smoked with them, using Big White's Mandan tobacco. Big White, a Mandan, spoke to these Arikaras about their differences, and hoped to return to the friendly terms they had been on before. A visiting Cheyenne Chief said that it was the fault of both tribes. The Arikaras agreed.

When they got to the next Arikara village, it was a different story. They greeted the Corps, but when they saw Big White, they threatened him. Clark had to warn that the Corps would defend him to the last man. Then all calmed down and the Arikara chief said that it was the Sioux, not his Arikara people, that had killed the Mandans . Then they all ate corn, beans and squash before proceeding on.

There was more good news about Lewis on the 22nd, when Clark wrote that he had walked a little for the first time, and he, (as the doctor), has discontinued the tent in the hole the ball came out. I assume the entering hole still needed more healing.

At the Arikara village, they found another man that had been with Warfington when the barge went down river. This man, whom Clark called Rokey, requested to be taken down to

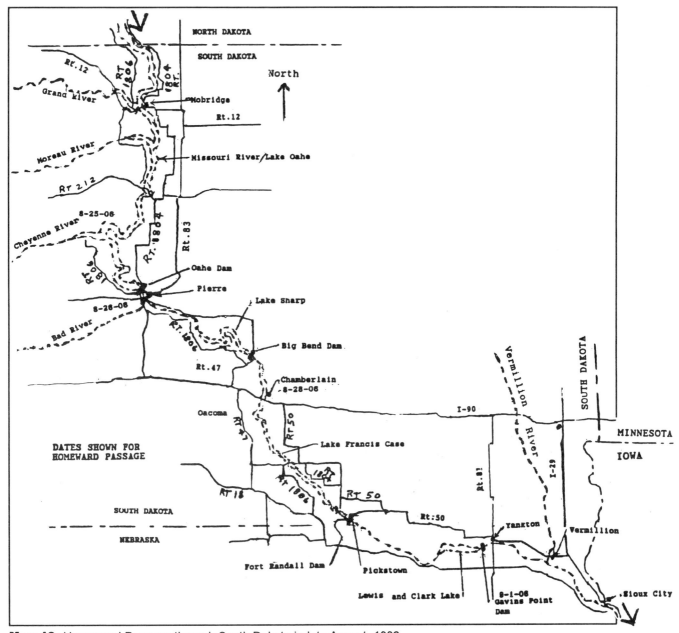

Map 19: Homeward Passage through South Dakota in late August, 1806.

St. Louis, and the captains approved. Now there were 38 in the party.

When they reached the Cheyenne River, they were getting near to the place where they had seen the last of the Teton Sioux on the way upriver. They took noon observations of the Cheyenne confluence on August 25th, and then proceeded on to below their encampment of September 29, 1804. It was near a large village of the Arikaras that had been destroyed by the Sioux. The next morning they passed the Bad River at 9 am, which is across the Missouri from Pierre, South Dakota. This is where the first confrontation with the Teton Sioux had occurred two years before. This time they saw no Sioux and they sped by, covering 60 miles that day, besides taking time to stop at Loisel's Fort, which was empty.

The next day Lewis became too eager and walked so far on a sand bar that he had a setback in his healing process, and was "very unwell all night." However, a few days later Clark said he was healing slowly again.

Chamberlain, South Dakota was passed on August 28, and they camped a short distance below, at what they called Pleasant Camp, the same as the Plum Camp of two years before. One of the best camps we can remember is at Chamberlain, and we always make a point to stay a few days when we are in that vicinity. There was an abundance of game here and the wives of Chief Big White and Jessome picked more plums than they could eat in two days. There were no mosquitos here either, which added to their pleasure. There were great herds of buffalo on both sides of the river.

The Fields brothers and Shannon went out hunting early on August 30th, and were to meet the rest at an appointed place down river. Meanwhile, near the appointed place, they saw 20 Indians on the opposite (eastern) bank. Then 80 or 90 more came out of the woods and signaled with their guns to which the Corps did the same. Clark wasn't sure what tribe they were from, so he went to their side of the river with three of his men that were French, for interpreters to talk to them. He went to a sand bar close enough to hear them. When they said that their chief was Black Buffalo, he recognized the name of the chief of the Teton Sioux he had had trouble with two years before at the Bad River.

Then he chewed them out. He had probably been waiting for the opportunity for a long time. He called them bad people, and said if they crossed to the side his party was on, that they would certainly be killed. They asked for some of the corn they saw in Clark's boat, but he refused. Some of them swam over to Clark's position and he told them that he hadn't forgotten the way he was treated by them, or of the other Whites and Indians they had robbed. He told them he knew about their people being on the way to fight with the Mandans and Hidatsas, but that they would be whipped, because those people had plenty of powder and shot and now had a cannon with which to defend themselves. All this time Clark was anxious for the safety of the Fields brothers and Shannon, but to his joy they soon hove in sight. Then they proceeded on for about 6 miles and camped on an island in the middle of the river. It was a wet and windy camp but it was protection from being disturbed by the Sioux.

This camp had no protection from the wind and the rain, however, when a storm hit them before midnight. It broke the ropes holding the two small canoes, but the men got them back on the island with difficulty. Then one of the catamarans with Wiser and Willard in it broke loose, but two men were not enough to handle it, and they were blown onto the eastern shore. Clark sent Ordway with six men in the other catamaran, which Clark called a small pirogue, to rescue them. At 2 am, the wind slackened a little, and they all returned to the island. At daylight they examined their arms and proceeded on. They couldn't have gotten much sleep that night. Sleep or no sleep, they traveled 70 miles that day, the last day in August. The last part of the day they were passing, on the right hand side, what is now Nebraska.

Nine Indians of the Yankton tribe appeared on the bank on September 1st, and Clark thought they might be Teton Sioux. They signaled for the canoes to stop, but Clark ignored them. After he passed he heard them shooting at something, and he thought it might be at his hunters, Reubin and Joe Fields and Shannon, who were in that area. Determined to defend his men, he took 15 of his party and ran up toward where they were. At the same time, Lewis hobbled up the bank, leading the rest to form a defensive position. Clark found that the Indians were only shooting at an old keg and that they were friendly Yankton Sioux. All had a smoke together before proceeding on. This was on present day Lewis and Clark Lake, formed by the lowest of the Missouri River dams, this one near Yankton, South Dakota. Exactly two years before this, on September 1, 1804, they passed this same place on their way upriver. They camped that night opposite to the former Calumet Bluff council site, where Gavins Point Dam is now. Today there are many campgrounds, right on the river, in that area. It is a vacationers mecca.

The Corps had an interesting meeting on the 3rd, with a James Aird, who was passing upriver on a trading mission. He had some news of what had been happening in the world and the nation. He told of General Wilkinson being Governor of Louisiana, stationed at St. Louis, and his troubles with the Spanish at Natchitoches, and the soldiers at St. Louis being sent south to help him. Aird told of the Burr/Hamilton duel, and of a British ship firing on an American ship and killing a seaman. They also got a barrel of flour and tobacco from Mr Aird. Clark's best report that day is that his friend Capt. Lewis was able to walk around with ease. This was 23 days after being shot.

They passed the Big Sioux River (at Sioux City, Iowa),and reached Floyd's grave at noon on September 4th. Here they found that the Indians had unearthed the grave, and buried a chief's son in the grave with Floyd, but did not fully cover it up. The Corps covered it, and then proceeded on to a sand bar below, to camp and dry their baggage. This was near their 6 day long camp of two years before, when they were looking for Indians to have a counsel with, and waiting for Drewyer to get back with Reed, the deserter.

Since the 4th of July, 1805, when they drank the last of their liquor, after completing the Great Falls portage, they hadn't had any whiskey. Their drought was about to be over on September 6th, when they met a trading bateau of August Chouteau, under Mr Henry

DeLorn, and the captains purchased a gallon of the stuff, and then DeLorn wouldn't take any pay for it. (That is about 3 ounces for each man) Some of the men traded their leather shirts for linen ones, and beaver for what Clark called "Corse hats." DeLorn was on the way to trade with the Yanktons, and Clark advised him not to have anything to do with the Teton Sioux.

They passed present day towns of Onawa, Iowa on the 5th, Blair, Neb. on the 7th, and Council Bluffs/Omaha on the 8th, and they camped at their old White Catfish Camp, 12 miles above the Platte River confluence. Big White, the squaws and children were getting travel weary, and Clark tells on the 6th, about the children crying. Clark was especially interested in the rate of evaporation, for he notes that many rivers had run into the Missouri as they came down, but the river hadn't become any larger. He also noticed that 9/10ths of the water in his inkwell evaporates, so that is where the river water is going, too.

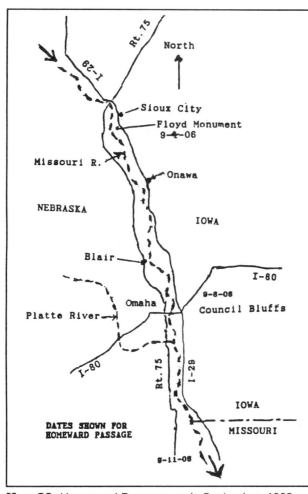

Map 20: Homeward Passage, early September, 1806.

More boats were met going upriver; on the 10th, they met a Mr. La Frost headed for the Platte River, who gave them another bottle of whiskey; and then a Mr. LaCroix, who was headed for the Omahas. On the 12th they met one of Chouteau's boats bound for the Platte River, and another to trade with the Omahas. Later that day they came to Clark's old friend, Robert McClellan, who had with him Gravelines and Dorion, both of whom had been interpreters for the captains. Gravelines had escorted an Indian chief to Washington, and the Indian died when he was there. These two interpreters had been sent by Jefferson to explain the death to the Arikaras, and to bring gifts to mollify their sorrows. History tells us that it didn't appease them at all. The Arikaras were to give traders trouble for some time after that.

I am glad I read Clark's entry for September 13th, for he had just received some chocolate from McClellan. Suddenly he found himself "very unwell," and a little chocolate in a pint of water gave him great relief. So now I have been following his example. If it was good for

106

Clark it will be good for me. The fact that I am a chocaholic has nothing to do with it. It was a good thing that McClellan had given him that chocolate, just in time. They camped that night south of present day St. Joseph, MO.

Besides the chocolate, they got more whiskey from McClellan, and then some more from three large boats on the 14th. That night, north of the Kansas River, even though they were camping in the area that the Kansas Indians stole from the traders boats, Clark wrote that they "received a dram and Sung Songs until 11 o'clock at night in the greatest of harmoney." They weren't home yet, but they were starting to feel that home wasn't far away. Apparently, the thieves stayed away that night. Or maybe they were there drinking with the Corps!

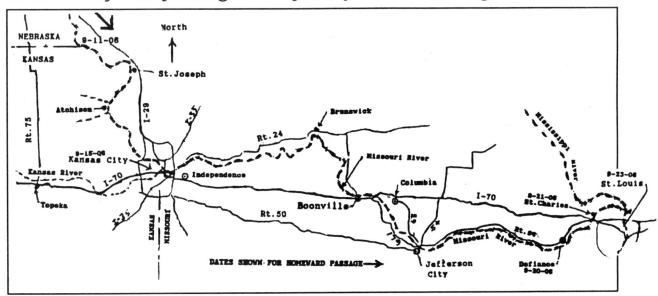

Map 21: Homeward Passage, the final leg and the celebrations or their triumphant return.

As they passed, on September 15th, the spot where the city of Kansas City, MO. is now, Clark described it as being a very good place for a fort. They stopped so the men could pick custard apples which grew there and the men were very fond of. But they did not like the weather that he said was "disagreeably worm." The men paddled slowly to keep from getting overheated, because they were used to the coolness of higher latitudes.

They passed another northward bound party on the 16th, and then a John McClallan on the 17th, who was a friend of Capt. Lewis. He had big plans to buy horses from the Indians at the Platte River, and go overland to trade with Santa Fe. The Corps traded their corn for biscuits, sugar, and more chocolate and whiskey.

Three of the men got sore eyes and couldn't see to paddle, which they thought had been brought on by the sun, so, on September 20th, they had to abandon the catamaran that Clark's small party of 9 had built up on the Yellowstone River. The sore eyes might have been caused by the toxic skin of the fruit they had been eating, which were papaws they had picked since they passed the Kansas River. When they rubbed the sweat on their foreheads after handling the fruit, it got in their eyes. At least that is a theory that I have read about.

When they saw cows on the bank, they shouted for joy, because they were nearing the first white village they had seen for 2 years and 4 months. This was the village of Charrette which they last saw on May 25, 1804. There were 5 trading boats there which gave them a three gun salute. Several of the men stayed with the villagers; the captains stayed in the tent of a trader. All were surprised to see the Corps of Discovery, for the rest of the world thought they would never come back. But they had suddenly returned to the land of speculation, for the merchant there made them pay 8 dollars for 2 gallons of whiskey, which they thought was an imposition. They were much interested in the Schenectady design of the traders boats, (bateaux) which were 30 feet long and 8 feet wide, flat bottomed, and pointed both ends. Something new in the marine industry.

The next day, September 21st at 4 pm, they arrived at St. Charles, to a warm reception. That night the whole party slept in houses. Real houses. Maybe with beds and bedsheets! Even pillows!

The next morning they went to Fort Bellefontaine, which had been built on the south side of the Missouri River, only 3 miles from the Mississippi River. It was built in 1805, when the Corps was in the Rocky Mountains, and besides being a fort, it was a factory which made goods to be sold to the Indians at a reasonable rate. Here Col. Hunt and Lieut. Peters kindly received them all. General Wilkinson's wife was there, but very sickly. She died the following winter. The General was down at the Natchitoches confrontation. The captains purchased clothes for Chief Big White (Shaheke) at that factory.

The last day of the trip they proceeded on to the Mississippi River, and across to Camp Dubois, where they had commenced this great expedition. There they found their former winter training camp had been turned into a plantation by a widowed woman. Then they proceeded down the Mississippi River to St. Louis where they arrived at 12 o'clock on September 23, 1806. The party fired off their guns in a salute to the town. The voyage of the Corps of Discovery had finished.

CONCLUSION

The return of the explorers to St. Louis was exciting for the city, and they feted the men at celebrations, parties, and balls. After all, these men had been given up for dead, and now they had shown up with information that enlightened the world about the northwest. They had won the race to the Pacific Ocean. Many letters were written by Lewis and Clark to the President and other important American leaders. Even leaders in Europe read about it, and made visits to St. Louis to learn about the exploration and to make explorations of their own, with the permission of U.S. authorities. Clark settled down in St. Louis and entertained many of Europe's royalty, besides prominent men of the U.S. and delegations of Indians.

Reporters were probably everywhere, because at that time more and more people were learning to read. When I was in Chamberlain, South Dakota, I saw, in a library, some very old children's books that told the story of Lewis and Clark. The 1904 World's Fair was in St. Louis, to commemorate the 100th anniversary of the expedition and the Louisiana Purchase. When I was in 5th grade in Massachusetts, in about 1927, I studied all about the exploration. Our country was still talking about it then. But now, people who do not live along the trail have forgotten it, and some have never even heard of it.

The men of the Corps of Discovery all received double pay for their time, and as a reward, they were given land grants to encourage them to become settlers. A similar land grant had been given to Revolutionary War Veterans. Lewis was made Governor of the Territory of Louisiana and Clark became Superintendent of Indian Affairs for Louisiana Territory. (Both of these positions were for Upper Louisiana.) Lewis became mentally ill in 1809, and on the way to Washington, was killed or committed suicide in Tennessee. Clark died at his home in St. Louis in 1838 after a productive and fruitful life. Their later lives are another story, tragic for Lewis; enriching for Clark.

The diaries of the Corps of Discovery written by the two captains were not published until 1814, but the Gass journal was published in July, 1807. The Ordway, Whitehouse, and Floyd diaries are printed, and parts of Shannon's. Pryor's and Frazer's have not been found. Willard might have written one too.

Most of the information I have put into this book I have taken from Gary Moulton's wonderful volumes on The Lewis and Clark Journals. As far as bringing readers up to date on the history of the United States for 30 years before and after the expeditions, the notes in his books are as enlightening as the journals themselves. If we were living at that time and knew what was going on in the world, the journals would be easy to understand. But reading them now, without the continual clarification that Moulton's notes add to the story, they would be much less interesting. Thanks to Gary Moulton and the University of Nebraska that published the books.

Another book that has helped me is Donald Jackson's collection of the letters of the Lewis and Clark Expedition from 1783 to 1854. Various leaders of our nation that wrote letters about it's preparation for, and its results afterwards, are in the book, and also what was being written while the expedition was taking place.

I was fortunate to be able to take the Gary Moulton books out of the University of South Florida Library for long enough periods to take them with me over the Lewis and Clark Trail, several times. These have broadened our understanding of the trail as we followed it.

Of course, the best way of keeping in touch with Lewis and Clark is to read, 4 times every year, what the leading scholars of today are finding out and writing, about the old trail. This is in WPO (We Proceeded On), the publication of the Lewis and Clark Trail Heritage Foundation, Inc., P. O. Box 3434, Great Falls, MT (discovery@lewisandclark.org) and you only have to join the Foundation to have it delivered to you. I heartily recommend it to anyone.

In my library I have John Bakeless's <u>Journals of Lewis and Clark</u> which skip some of the daily entries but are very helpful, Harold Howard's <u>Sacajawea</u>, and Dayton Duncan's <u>Out West</u>, who is an excellent writer and must be an interesting fellow. I received a lot of help from these books. Every writer has added a new way of looking at the expedition. Next, I want to read new books by Steve Ambrose and by Jim Ronda, who are known to be very accurate and well informed about Lewis and Clark. I have heard them both speak, and I hope to again.

I hope this book reaches campers (tents or RV's) or any tourists who are looking for an interesting place to go on their next vacation. We have enjoyed the trail and hope you do too.

Thanks, Lena, for being patient with me while I have devoted my time to this writing. Thanks to Sharon Ostermann for the retyping and correcting that she has done on this book. Her hard work and the encouragement of her husband, my long-time friend, Joe, have helped make my work easier. Thanks also to her brother-in-law, Andy Safko, who prepared my pictures for being copied into the book. My brother Ben, both an engineer and avid reader, gave lots of valuable suggestions that added clarity to the contents. And thanks to Sue Gibson for a thorough job of proofreading. Walter Kruschwitz got me straightened out early in my writing and I appreciate it.